Classic Love Comics Retold!

TRUER THAN TRUE ROMANCE

by Jeanne Martinet

WATSON-GUPTILL PUBLICATIONS • NEW YORK

Acknowledgements

There are numerous people who have contributed to the making of this book; I hope they will all forgive me for not trying to list all their names here. Most of all I would like to thank Jason Harootunian, Trent Duffy and Steve Korté for their help and unceasing encouragement. Who needs true love when you have such great editors?

For Watson-Guptill Publications:
Senior Acquisitions Editor: Candace Raney
Editor: Jacqueline Ching
Production Manager: Ellen Greene
Marketing Manager: Ali T. Kokmen
Cover and interior design: Michelle Gengaro

For DC Comics:
Editor: Steve Korté (Licensed Publishing)
Managing Editor: Trent Duffy (Licensed Publishing)

First published in 2001 by Watson-Guptill Publications,
a division of BPI Communications, Inc.
770 Broadway, New York, NY 10003
www.watsonguptill.com

Library of Congress Cataloging-in-Publication Data
        Truer than true romance: classic love comics retold / by Jeanne Martinet.
            p.   cm.
        Ten DC Comics romance stories, with new words in the captions and balloons.
        ISBN 0-8230-8438-8
        1. Love—Comic books, strips, etc. I. Title.
        PN6726.M35 2001
        741.5′973—dc21   2001017933

Printed in the United States of America

First printing, 2001

1 2 3 4 5 6 7 8 9 / 09 08 07 06 05 04 03 02 01

Contents

If It's Raining, It Must Be Love

My single friends and I have many theories about why we have been unsuccessful in our search for True Love. Depending on our mood, we blame ourselves, society, the media, our parents, our exes, our therapists, our hairstylists, lingerie manufacturers, genetics, geography, demography, or evil spirits (one woman I know swears her dead grandmother is ruining her love life from the other side). But after unearthing an old box of childhood memorabilia from the back of my closet, I finally succeeded in identifying the real culprit: romance comics.

Aha, I thought, as I was rereading the innocent-looking, pretty stories in my dog-eared issues of *Young Romance*, *Falling in Love*, and *Heart Throbs*, no wonder I tend to fall in love at first sight! No wonder I love going out in thunderstorms (which is where all the really steamy romance comic moments take place) and yet am always so surprised when the rain plasters my hair down flat. I am similarly shocked at what crying does to my looks — it doesn't seem right at all that my eyes should get so red and puffy. Shouldn't they stay beautiful and clear, with perfectly shaped tears suspended dramatically from the corners?

It's obvious to me now that romance comics infused my young brain with many strange notions about dating and love. For instance, I have always felt that men should drive swanky convertibles and that several long kisses should lead directly to a heartfelt declaration of love. And *of course* I associate birds with romance. Who doesn't? The mere sight of a flock of birds — especially sea gulls — makes my heart yearn for something in a thump-thump kind of way. I don't know why, but in these comics there are birds *everywhere* — flying around the couple's heads, following their car, perched on the windowsill outside the office where the heroine is taking dictation from her handsome boss. I certainly never saw any birds outside *my* window when I worked in an office. But I am sure that if I had had a handsome boss from whom I took dictation, I would never have married him, because according to the comics I am destined to marry someone from my small home town in the Midwest (which is a really frightening thought as I didn't even grow up in the Midwest). Romance comics showed me that love is more important than career, that women should never chase men, and that only females cry. Even worse: They instilled in me a serious predilection for bright colors. I have way too much red and yellow in my closets. I adore people with bright blue or bright orange hair.

I began reading these semi-sexy fairy tales for girls at the impressionable age of ten. What I didn't realize at the time was that the stories—from the advent of the genre in 1947 up until it petered out in the mid-70s—were written by men. This is undoubtedly the reason for the comics' sexist sensibility—and for the fact that everyone in romance comics has a perfect body, that the men are *always* taller than the girls and the handsome heroes are never ever bald. I doubt the writers themselves were exactly alpha men; they were most likely shy, middle-aged nerdy types. Maybe this explains one of the most common plots in the romance comics, in which the boring, steady guy triumphs in love over the exciting, charming ambitious guy. Nice guys finish first. Aggressive girls never got the man. No one had sex before wedlock. No one got pregnant.

There were also advice columns in most romance comics. These too were written by men, posing as experienced and attractive women. What does a man pretending to be a woman say to a young girl? Mostly incredibly perceptive things like "Ask your mother," and "Go out with boys only in groups."

I felt it was time to begin to rectify this warped vision of romance, to undo some of the psychological damage done.

I kept wondering what these stories would be like if they were written by a woman today. Hell—what if they were written by *me*? When *I* go to an airport, *I* am much more concerned with my luggage than I am with picking up a pilot (see "Carry-On Girl!"). Far from having to deal with two men fighting over me, I can't seem to find a straight one to even date (see "Loving Gay Men!"). And I am much more likely to have to choose between my married lover and my therapist ("My Heart Said Yes—But My Therapist Said No!") than between a rich man and a poor man.

And so here are ten romance comics rewritten for your romantic enlightenment—along with some brand-new romance advice columns (I think readers will find Dee Pressen a lot more accurate than the old advice columnists—even if she *is* a bit of a downer). All of the stories are newly created; I took my inspiration from the art itself, completely tossing out the old captions and word balloons.

As a child I used to like to eat candy while I read romance comics, which is probably why I now have to have dessert when I go on a date. For reading *Truer Than True Romance*, I recommend something more along the lines of a dry martini—with a twist.

Jeanne Martinet

From *Young Romance* #128 (February–March 1964). Illustrated by Mike Sekowsky and Bernard Sachs.

Original plot: Alice is torn between a man with a secure financial future and a handsome marina bum. No surprise, she chooses the handsome marina bum in the end, only to discover that he is independently wealthy (of course) and has his own boat.

I HAD BEEN IN COUNSELING FOR TEN YEARS, TRYING TO GET OVER MY OBSESSION WITH MARRIED MEN, AND HERE I WAS ABOUT TO MAKE THE SAME MISTAKE ONCE AGAIN...

MY HEART SAID YES – BUT MY THERAPIST SAID NO!

CHARLIE WAS MY BOSS AT THE RESTAURANT. I COULD TELL HE WANTED TO SLEEP WITH ME, AND EVEN THOUGH HE WAS MARRIED, I WAS FLATTERED...

ALICE, HOW ABOUT A LONELY DRIVE IN THE COUNTRY TOMORROW?

SURE, CHARLIE! I NEVER HAVE ANYTHING TO DO ANYWAY.

I KNEW IT WAS DANGEROUS FOR ME TO SEE HIM OUTSIDE OF WORK, BUT HE WAS JUST SUCH A NICE GUY...

SO WHAT'S YOUR *WIFE* DOING TODAY?

LOOK, SHE DOESN'T UNDERSTAND ME. OKAY? SO LET'S NOT TALK ABOUT THE OLD BAG.

YOU'VE GOT A GREAT BODY, ALICE. WHOEVER GETS YOU IS GOING TO BE A LUCKY MAN!

THANK YOU, CHARLIE. AND MAY I SAY THAT YOUR WIFE IS LUCKY TOO.

ONE OF THE THINGS I LOVED ABOUT CHARLIE WAS HIS ASSERTIVENESS...

LOOK, SHUT UP ALREADY ABOUT MY WIFE!!

SORRY.

I WAS SO CONFUSED BY MY GROWING FEELINGS THAT I ASKED MY THERAPIST, ROGER, TO COME TO THE RESTAURANT AND SECRETLY CHECK CHARLIE OUT...

LOOK AT THAT HUNKY GUY OVER THERE, TALKING TO CHARLIE.

THAT'S MY SHRINK. I WANTED HIS OPINION ON MEN...ER... I MEAN, ON THE MENU.

ROGER ALWAYS TRIED TO MAKE ME FEEL BETTER ABOUT MYSELF...

YOU SURE LOOK HOT IN THAT OUTFIT, ALICE.

OH, YOU AND YOUR ETERNAL EGO-BUILDING! I LOOK LIKE HEIDI ON HORMONES IN THIS THING.

2

I COULDN'T WAIT TO ASK HIM WHAT HE THOUGHT OF CHARLIE....

WELL, *DU-UH*! HE'S ANOTHER MARRIED ASSHOLE WHO WILL BREAK YOUR HEART. WHAT'S GOOD TO EAT HERE?

THE LAMB IS SUPERB. AND YOU CAN CERTAINLY AFFORD IT!

ROGER NEVER STOPPED WORKING ON BOUNDARY ISSUES WITH ME...

YOU CERTAINLY DON'T EXPECT ME TO PAY FOR MY OWN LUNCH AFTER I CAME ALL THE WAY DOWN HERE!

THIS DOESN'T SEEM FAIR.

HIS LUNCH WAS GOING TO COST ME A DAY'S WAGES. I WISHED I HAD SUGGESTED SOUP...

I THOUGHT YOU MIGHT LIKE A COMPLIMENTARY COFFEE, SEEING AS I HAVE TO PAY.

THIS CHARLIE GUY CERTAINLY PUTS YOU ON EDGE. OR IS IT PMS?

BUT BEFORE ROGER LEFT...

HERE COMES THE MAN WHO KNOWS ALL YOUR MOST SECRET THOUGHTS.

I BET HE DOESN'T KNOW I SPIT IN HIS COFFEE.

HE SURPRISED ME...

WHAT'S THIS, DOCTOR? DO YOU NEED CHANGE OR WHAT?

I THOUGHT MAYBE I WAS BEING UNFAIR. AFTER ALL, LUNCH *WAS* GREAT. HERE'S HALF.

AS HE WALKED AWAY FROM ME, I FELT GIDDY... NOT JUST THE USUAL PROZAC GIDDY, BUT *REALLY* GIDDY...

WOW! I NEVER EXPECTED HIM TO BE SO GENEROUS! AFTER ALL THOSE MISSED APPOINTMENTS HE MADE ME PAY FOR.

3

I SUDDENLY REALIZED I HAD NEVER SEEN HIM FROM THE BACK...

HAVE YOU NOTICED THAT YOUR SHRINK HAS A FAIRLY NICE BUTT ON HIM?

NOT UNTIL *NOW*, DOTTY!

THE NEXT DAY, ROGER CAME BACK FOR LUNCH. I BEGAN TO SEE HIM IN A WHOLE NEW LIGHT...

GOSH. I CAN'T BELIEVE HE SMOKES. IT'S DISGUSTING, BUT AT THE SAME TIME STRANGELY COMPELLING.

HEY DOLL-BABY.

HE WAS ALWAYS TRYING NEW FORMS OF THERAPY ON ME, BUT I COULDN'T BELIEVE WHAT HE SAID NEXT...

LOOK. SINCE YOUR SOCIAL LIFE IS SO PATHETIC--AND BOY, I SHOULD KNOW--HOW ABOUT LETTING ME TAKE YOU OUT AND SHOW YOU A GOOD TIME?

WHY, ROGER!

WHERE DOES CHARLIE TAKE YOU?

USUALLY FOR A DRIVE SOMEWHERE.

THEN I'LL TAKE YOU FOR A WALK.

THE NEXT DAY WOULD HAVE BEEN PERFECT IF I HADN'T BEEN WEARING HIGH HEELS...

SORRY ROGER, I HAVE TO STOP FOR A MOMENT. THESE BLISTERS ARE KILLING ME!

IT'S ALWAYS *SOMETHING* WITH YOU.

WE WALKED FOR HOURS. I SAW A SIDE OF MY THERAPIST I HADN'T SEEN DURING OUR SESSIONS...

WHAT A PROFILE! I DON'T THINK I'VE EVER LOOKED AT THIS SIDE OF YOUR FACE.

I DON'T SHOW IT TO JUST ANYONE. YOU'RE MY FAVORITE PATIENT, ALICE.

4

WHEN MY FOOT PAIN GOT REALLY BAD, WE STOPPED TO EAT IN A DIMLY LIT DINER...

ALICE, I'M GOING TO DO SOMETHING SPECIAL FOR YOU.

FOR ME? I HOPE IT WON'T COST EXTRA.

MY RESPONSE SEEMED TO INFURIATE HIM....

STOP THINKING ABOUT MONEY AND START THINKING ABOUT YOUR LIFE! I WANT TO SHOW YOU WHAT IT CAN BE LIKE WITH A REAL MAN! A SINGLE MAN!

GOLLY!

AS HIS LIPS MET MINE, I FELT A STRANGE RUSH OF EMOTIONS....

THIS IS SO WEIRD.

I'M READY TO GO ALL OUT TO HELP YOU, ALICE!

I'VE ALWAYS TRUSTED HIM. AND HE DOES HAVE THAT CUTE BUTT. BUT I DON'T KNOW....

THAT NIGHT I TOSSED AND TURNED....

ROGER...CHARLIE...ROGER...CHARLIE... ROGER...DOTTY---WAIT! WHAT AM I SAYING?!

I WANTED TO BELIEVE IN ROGER, BUT CHARLIE STILL HAD A STRANGE POWER OVER ME...

...SO THEN SHE SAYS TO ME, WHY CAN'T YOU HELP THE KIDS WITH THEIR HOMEWORK, AND I SAY TO HER, I DON'T DO HOME-WORK, I DO HOME-REST!

COME OVER HERE AND KISS ME, YOU BIG STRONG THING YOU.

5

HONEYPOT, YOU'RE DRIVING ME CRAZY. MEET ME AT THE PINK FLAMINGO HOTEL IN ONE HOUR.

ARE YOU GOING TO LEAVE YOUR WIFE?

DON'T BE RIDICULOUS. WHADDYA THINK THIS IS, A SAPPY FAIRY TALE?

GOD, I LOVE YOU.

DOTTY HELPED ME GET READY FOR MY BIG ROMANTIC RENDEZVOUS. I WAS EXCITED AND TERRIFIED ALL AT ONCE...

I THINK IT'S GREAT, AL. MAYBE WE'LL BOTH GET RAISES!

STRICTLY SPEAKING, IT'S ADULTERY. BUT OH WELL.

AS FATE WOULD HAVE IT, WHEN THE DOOR OF THE TAXI I WAS ABOUT TO TAKE TO THE PINK FLAMINGO OPENED, THERE WAS ROGER...

OH SHIT.

TAXI!

OF COURSE ROGER WANTED ME TO CANCEL MY DATE WITH CHARLIE....

HOW DID YOU KNOW I WAS ABOUT TO TAKE THE BIG PLUNGE?

YOU SILLY GOOFBALL! I KNOW YOU SO WELL. I KNOW WHAT YOU'RE GOING TO DO BEFORE YOU DO. DON'T GO.

6

I HATED SEEING ROGER'S DISAPPROVAL, BUT SOMEHOW THE GUILT TRIP HE LAID ON ME MADE ME HORNY AS HELL...

I WANT TO GO.

SLEEP WITH ME INSTEAD.

SUDDENLY I HAD A MOMENT OF CLARITY...

N-NO, ROGER, I WON'T. I'VE BEEN UNDER YOUR THERAPEUTIC SPELL LONG ENOUGH. IN FACT, I'M LEAVING THERAPY--LEAVING YOU!!

YOU DON'T KNOW WHAT YOU'RE SAYING. YOU'RE NOT READY. COME IN ON TUESDAY AND WE'LL TALK ABOUT IT.

I TOLD ROGER NO, AND THAT I WOULD PROBABLY STILL BE AT THE PINK FLAMINGO ANYWAY. IT WAS HARD TO WALK AWAY...

I'VE MADE HIM ANGRY. I WONDER HOW I'LL GET MY PROZAC NOW....

I GOT IN THE TAXI AND TOLD HIM TO TAKE ME TO THE PINK FLAMINGO HOTEL...

WHAT HAVE I DONE? HOW CAN I POSSIBLY BEAR MY TUESDAYS, WEDNESDAYS AND THURSDAYS WITHOUT SEEING ROGER?

I'VE GOT TO FACE FACTS. I MAY BE *ATTRACTED* TO CHARLIE, BUT I'M *ADDICTED* TO ROGER....

THIS IS IT, LADY.

WAIT! I'VE CHANGED MY MIND. DRIVE ME TO WHERE ALL THE DOCTORS AND LAWYERS KEEP THEIR BOATS!

7

15

EXCUSE ME. DO YOU BY ANY CHANCE KNOW WHERE A PSYCHIATRIST NAMED ROGER MIGHT BE?

SURE. BIG YACHT DOWN THERE. EVERYBODY KNOWS "ROMEO ROGER."

THAT YOU, SUSIE?

NO, IT'S ME, ALICE! I COULDN'T GO THROUGH WITH IT! YOU MEAN TOO MUCH TO ME!

OF COURSE I'LL SLEEP WITH YOU, ROGER. JUST SAY YOU WON'T CHARGE ME FOR IT.

I'M GLAD YOU'VE COME TO YOUR SENSES, BABY. I KNOW HOW TO TAKE CARE OF YOU. LET'S LIVE TOGETHER.

ROGER'S BOAT WAS HUGE. IT FELT RIGHT THAT I WOULD BE LIVING ON IT, AS MY SESSIONS HAD HELPED PAY FOR IT...

SIR, THERE'S ANOTHER LADY ON THE DOCK WHO IS DEMANDING TO SEE YOU. SHALL I DELAY SETTING SAIL?

DON'T BE SILLY, MAN. I'VE GOT MY LADY RIGHT HERE. SHE'LL BE MY ONLY FOCUS FOR A WHILE. AND WE'VE GOT TO GET HER AWAY FROM THE TEMPTATION OF THE PINK FLAMINGO, ASAP!

AS WE STARTED OUT TO SEA, I THREW MY ARMS AROUND ROGER. NOW HE WOULD ALWAYS BE MY THERAPIST! I HAD BROKEN MY SELF-DESTRUCTIVE PATTERN WITH MARRIED MEN, AND HAD EMBARKED ON A WHOLE NEW KIND OF RELATIONSHIP...

8

TESS T.

Dear Tess,

My younger sister is going to be married in a few months. She has been engaged for two years, and during all that time I naturally assumed that I would be the maid of honor at the wedding. Now she has told me that she would like me to be one of her bridesmaids, and that she has asked her best friend to be the maid of honor.

It's true that I haven't been very close to my sister in the past few years, because I have been working away from home. In fact, I've only seen her twice since she become engaged. Even so, I think she should have shown more consideration toward me. I don't know if I ought to go along with just being a bridesmaid or if I should teach her a lesson and refuse.

Naomi
Montgomery, Ala.

Dear Naomi,

Oh by all means, teach her a lesson. There's nothing like ruining your sister's wedding. I think you should not only refuse to be a bridesmaid, but also refuse to attend, period. In fact, maybe you could pour gasoline on the cake when no one is looking. Or put Superglue in her shoes so she has to wear them throughout the honeymoon.

While you're at it, Sis, why don't you go torture some cats and dig up your neighbor's petunias? That sounds like something you might find fun.

Tess T.

♥　♥　♥

Dear Tess,

A few days ago my best friend Shelly asked me to help her plan a surprise party for her boyfriend Howie. There's only one problem. Howie has been secretly dating *me* for a month and intends to break up with Shelly this weekend. Should I play dumb and help her with the party or should I tell her she's wasting her time? I really don't want to see her get hurt more than she has to.

Party Pooper
Pittsburgh, Pa.

Dear Party Pooper,

I have to tell you that I really feel for you. It can be so hard to be a teenager. And you certainly do have a very tough problem. That problem being, or course, that you are an immature, selfish, greedy backstabber, who wouldn't know the meaning of the word "friendship" if you had it tattooed over your stupid, cheating butt.

You've been fooling Shelly for this long—why stop now? Besides, I think a babe like you would have a swell time planning the party on the phone with her while sitting on Howie's lap. Then at the actual party, you could stand up and announce that you've stolen your best friend's boyfriend. Now that's a surprise party.

Tess T.

♥　♥　♥

Dear Tess,

This boy I know has asked me to a party at his parents' home in the country. Lots of kids I know are going. I'd really love to go, only it will probably last until very late. I'm afraid to ask my parents for permission 'cause they are liable to say I can't go. I'll die if I can't go! I'm thinking of telling my folks I am staying over at a girlfriend's house. Wouldn't that be better?

Lila
Dayton, Ohio

Dear Lila,

Or should I say "Lila the liar?" Let's see: Would it be better to lie to your parents about where you are going, and then stay at some horny boy's house where you will be drinking and God-knows-what-else until the sun comes up to shine on your pasty, debauched face? Definitely! This is a no-brainer. Go have fun. And Lila? Be sure to write me from prison when you get there.

Tess T.

From *Secret Hearts* #45 (February 1958). Illustrated by Bill Draut.

Original plot: A girl who works at the post office in a summer resort town develops a crush on a boy who comes every day looking for a letter from his girlfriend. To make him feel better, the postal worker decides to write him a letter pretending to be the girlfriend. The boy is angry at first at this trick but falls in love with the postal worker anyway.

NO ONE KNOWS HOW IT HAPPENED. SEA CREST USED TO BE A REAL SMART TOWN. THEN WE ALL GOT KIND OF SLOW. THEN I FELL FOR THIS GUY, PAUL. BUT I WAS JUST...
TOO DUMB FOR LOVE!
WAIT A MINUTE! ARE YOU TRYING TO TELL ME YOU WROTE THIS LETTER? HOW CAN YOU BE THIS DUMB?!

I LIKED TO WALK ON THE BEACH. I COULDN'T RE-MEMBER WHAT THE PRETTY WHITE BIRDS WERE CALLED, BUT I LIKED THE NOISE THEY MADE...

ON HOT DAYS EVERYONE WENT TO THE BEACH. BUT WE HAD FORGOTTEN A WHOLE BUNCH OF STUFF...

...LIKE HOW TO MAKE UMBRELLAS STAND UP IN THE SAND...

THE SUN IS REAL HOT. I WISH I HAD SOME SHADE.

MY JOB HAD SOMETHING TO DO WITH MAIL. I WASN'T REAL SURE WHAT I WAS SUPPOSED TO DO. I DID THE BEST I COULD...

THOSE FOR ME?

I'VE NO IDEA.

ONE DAY THIS STRANGER CAME IN. HE WAS REAL PRETTY. HE SAID HE WANTED TO ASK ME SOME QUESTIONS...

MAY I TALK TO YOU?

HE WAS FROM SOME PLACE CALLED THE E.P.A. IN D.C. I DIDN'T KNOW WHERE THAT WAS OR WHAT THAT SPELLED. BUT I LIKED HIS PRETTY EYES....

WHAT'S *WRONG* WITH YOU?

2

HIS NAME WAS PAUL. HE SAID HE HAD COME TO SEE WHAT WAS THE MATTER WITH THE PEOPLE IN SEA CREST...

WE'RE ALL OKAY. LET'S SEE: WHICH HOLE LOOKS LIKE IT WANTS TO HAVE MAIL THINGIES IN IT?

THE FUNNY THING WAS THAT TALKING TO ME SEEMED TO UPSET PAUL AFTER A WHILE...

THIS IS **SERIOUS.**

DO **YOU** KNOW WHERE I LIVE?

LOTS OF FOLKS HAD FORGOTTEN WHERE THEY LIVED. AT NIGHT AFTER WORK, THE TOWNSPEOPLE MOSTLY JUST MILLED AROUND IN A CONFUSED WAY...

SOMETIMES I HAD TO WALK FOR A REALLY, REALLY LONG TIME BEFORE I FOUND MY HOUSE. I DIDN'T MIND SO MUCH. EXCEPT SOMETIMES WHEN MY FEET GOT TIRED...

TAKE A RIGHT HERE, NO, LEFT... I'M GETTING CLOSE...WAIT... **WHERE** AM I TRYING TO GO?

PAUL CAME TO SEE ME EVERY DAY. THAT'S HOW COME I REMEMBERED HIS NAME WAS PAUL. HE STILL WANTED TO ASK ME THINGS. I STILL THOUGHT HE WAS PRETTY...

DO YOU KNOW YOUR **NAME?**

SORRY!

YOUR **ADDRESS?**

SORRY!

YOUR **SEX?**

SORRY!

3

PAUL ONCE ASKED ME IF I COULD WRITE. I DECIDED TO SURPRISE HIM...

I'LL COPY FROM A BOOK SO HE'LL THINK I'M SMART. I WANT HIM TO LIKE ME!

to download files from the hard drive

PAUL CAME IN. I COULD TELL HE WASN'T HAVING A GOOD DAY. HE LOOKED TIRED. BUT HE STILL LOOKED PRETTY...

YUMMY! I WISH I COULD REMEMBER HOW TO FLIRT WITH BOYS!

ALL I COULD DO WAS SMILE AND STARE AS I HANDED HIM MY THINGIE...

GOOD GIRL!

I WAS SO HAPPY PAUL SAID THAT TO ME! HE WENT OFF WITH THE PAPER, AND I WENT BACK TO MY CUSTOMERS...

MISS—DO YOU KNOW IF I AM MARRIED? I CAN'T SEEM TO REMEMBER...

I'LL ASK AROUND.

THAT EVENING WAS THE SAME AS IT ALWAYS WAS...

WHAT AM I DRESSED UP FOR? WHERE AM I GOING? WHAT TIME IS IT? HAVE I EATEN?

AND THE SAME THOUGHT HAUNTED ME...

I USED TO BE SMART.

4

THE NEXT DAY I GOT TO WORK SO LATE IT WAS CLOSED. OR MAYBE I WAS TOO EARLY. OR MAYBE IT WAS SUNDAY...

HOW WILL PAUL FIND ME?

CLOSED

SO I DECIDED TO PUT ON MY SUNDAY CLOTHES. I WENT TO THE BEACH...

PRETTY, PRETTY BIRDS...

SUDDENLY PAUL WAS BESIDE ME...

YOU IDIOT! YOU DIDN'T WRITE THIS LETTER! YOU COPIED IT FROM A COMPUTER MANUAL. HOW CAN YOU BE SO DUMB?!

I COULDN'T UNDERSTAND WHY HE WAS SO MAD! I DIDN'T KNOW WHAT A COMPUTER MANUAL WAS! I HAD ONLY TRIED TO PLEASE HIM...

IT MADE ME SO SAD THAT HE WAS SMART AND I WAS DUMB AND WE WOULD NEVER GET MARRIED OR ANYTHING THAT I STARTED CRYING...

OHH!! I AM TOO DUMB TO LIVE!

THE NEXT THING I KNEW HE WAS HOLDING MY HANDS. HE WAS SO NICE. AND SO PRETTY. I FORGOT WHAT WE WERE EVEN TALKING ABOUT...

DON'T CRY. I SWEAR TO YOU I'M GOING TO GET TO THE BOTTOM OF THIS THING!

5

THAT'S WHEN PAUL STARTED TALKING FAST, LIKE HE WAS TRYING TO ADD SOMETHING UP. I ONLY WISHED I KNEW WHAT IT WAS...

I'VE TESTED THE DRINKING WATER, TAKEN RANDOM FOOD SAMPLES, TESTED FOR TOXINS IN THE AIR. I CAN *NOT* FIGURE OUT WHAT HAS *HAPPENED* TO THE PEOPLE IN THIS TOWN. BUT IT'S OBVIOUS THAT *BRAIN FUNCTION* IS IMPAIRED.

HE MARCHED OFF WITHOUT SAYING GOOD-BYE...

HE STILL SOUNDS SO MAD. HE DOESN'T LIKE DUMB PEOPLE. HE'S WALKING LIKE HE'S *MAD*. HE'S GOT A PRETTY REAR END. I LOVE HIM.

THAT NIGHT I DREAMED ABOUT PAUL. IN MY DREAM WE TALKED ABOUT ALL SORTS OF THINGS. AND I WAS AS SMART AS HIM...

YOU'RE AS SMART AS ME!

AND THEN HE GRABBED ME. HE KISSED ME REALLY HARD. IT FELT REALLY NEAT. I NEV-ER WANTED TO WAKE UP...

PHMMMPH MMPH, MMPH, MMPH

BUT THEN I DID WAKE UP! I WAS MAD I WOKE UP. I HATED NOT BEING ASLEEP, SINCE I WAS DUMB AGAIN...

DARN! HOW CAN I GET PAUL TO GRAB ME LIKE THAT WHEN I AM *AWAKE*?

I GOT DRESSED AND WENT TO THE BEACH. I FOUND PAUL TRYING TO CATCH FISH FROM THE OCEAN. SEEING HIM DOING THAT MADE ME REMEMBER SOMETHING...

I USED TO FISH IN THE SURF LIKE THAT. I THINK I USED TO COOK UP THE FISH FOR BREAKFAST. SO DID A LOT OF PEOPLE IN SEA CREST...

I FELT SUDDENLY VERY SCARED FOR PAUL...

WAIT! THERE'S SOMETHING *BAD* ABOUT THE *FISH*. I HAVE TO TELL PAUL TO *STOP*!

6

BUT THEN PAUL PUT HIS ARMS ON MINE AND I COULDN'T THINK OF ANYTHING BUT THAT MAYBE HE WOULD KISS ME REALLY HARD LIKE IN MY DREAM...

HE PULLED ME CLOSE SO OUR CHESTS WERE TOUCHING. IT WASN'T EXACTLY LIKE MY DREAM, BUT SORT OF...

WE WENT BACK TO HIS HOUSE TO COOK UP THE FISH HE HAD CAUGHT. I GOT A REALLY FUNNY FEELING AFTER I ATE THE FISH...

WE WENT SWIMMING THE NEXT DAY. IT MADE OUR SKIN TINGLE...

WE FISHED SOME MORE...

AT NIGHT WE STAYED ON THE BEACH. NEITHER ONE OF US COULD FIND OUR WAY HOME NOW...

WHAT'S HAPPENING TO PAUL? HE USED TO BE SO SMART. NOW HE'S MORE LIKE ME.

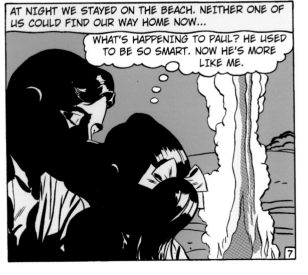

7

DURING THE DAY I STILL WENT TO WORK AT MY JOB. ONE DAY A MAIL THINGIE CAME THAT HAD THE WORD "PAUL" ON IT...

THIS COULD BE FOR *MY* PAUL. MAYBE THOSE PEOPLE IN THAT E-P-A TOWN WANT HIM BACK!

I WAS GOING TO THROW THE THINGIE AWAY BUT I FORGOT AND ENDED UP PUTTING IT IN ONE OF THE HOLES...

THERE'S A LOT OF ROOM LEFT IN *THIS* HOLE. THIS WILL HELP FILL IT UP...

LATER PAUL CAME IN TO HELP ME AT MY JOB. HE ASKED TO SEE SOME OF THE MAIL THINGIES...

CAN I SEE THOSE ONES?

HE MUST HAVE SEEN HIS NAME ON THE FRONT. THE NEXT THING I KNEW HE HAD OPENED IT...

NOW PAUL'S GOING TO GO AWAY! BACK TO WHERE HE CAME FROM! HE COULD NEVER LOVE ME ANYWAY! I'M WAY TOO DUMB!

THEN A REALLY GREAT THING HAPPENED. PAUL RIPPED UP THE LETTER INTO LITTLE PIECES! HE WASN'T GOING TO GO BACK TO E-P-A!

FOR SOME REASON, I CAN'T READ THIS THINGIE. BUT I DON'T *CARE*. YOU ARE SO *PRETTY*. I THINK I *LOVE* YOU!

8

HE KISSED ME HARD, LIKE IN MY DREAM. I WAS SO HAPPY! I WAS NOT TOO DUMB FOR LOVE! PAUL HAD BEEN TOO SMART FOR LOVE!

The End

ASK DR. MARY
Licensed Therapist*

Dear Dr. Mary,

I have a bad problem. I really like this cute guy. He dresses nicely and is extremely good-looking. But I'm too shy to talk to him. I have a friend who knows him, and she introduced him to me. Well, what I am trying to get at is that I love him very much and I would like to know how I can get him to like me too.

Hopeless

Dear Hopeless,

You've raised some hypersensitive issues, ones that many women in today's society share. I think part of the confusion stems from the fact that the friend who introduced you has a tendency toward triangulation, and she is manipulating your emotions in order to get to read aloud from her own family script. As for your relationship with this particular potential life partner, I think trying to dialogue with him would impact the situation enormously. You could try some rigorous role-playing and/or some inner-child interaction. However, it sounds most of all as if you suffer from very low self-esteem, probably due to being raised by substance-abusing, narcissist parents. You need some intensive one-on-one ego enhancement therapy, and you may want to ask your doctor about medication for Social Anxiety Disorder as well.

Have fun! These are your carefree years!

Dr. Mary

♥ ♥ ♥

> *Don't ask me, ask your inner child...*

Dear Dr. Mary,

I met a boy for the first time the other night, and really flipped for him. He seemed to flip for me too, because all he wanted to do was kiss me again and again. I didn't think it was wrong for him to kiss me occasionally that first evening, but that was all he wanted to do. I tried to make him understand that this was our first date, and that we should really get to know each other better before acting the way he wants to act.

The result? He never called back, and I am heartbroken. Should I call him up? And what should I say when I do?

Heartbroken

Dear Heartbroken,

Sexual dysfunction and fear of intimacy are quite common among American women. Often these complexes originate from same-sex parent inappropriate behavior modification you may have received as a child. You see, we all have these tapes playing in our head, and sometimes we don't like the music, or it's playing too loud.

Practice talking to yourself in a mirror before calling this boy, and during your languaging with him, be sure to avoid self-hating syntax and all use of the words "should," "I can't," or "pea-brain."

Be happy! Give your subconscious self a back rub!

Dr. Mary

(* in some U.S. states)

27

From *Falling in Love* #4 (February–March 1956). Illustrated by Tony Abruzzo and Bernard Sachs.

Original plot: Gail travels to the big city to visit her best friend Marjorie and promptly falls head over heels for Marjorie's fiancé. For a while Gail suffers from unrequited love, until at last the fiancé reveals his hankering for Gail. Marjorie graciously steps aside.

I DON'T KNOW HOW IT HAPPENED....ONE MINUTE I WAS TELLING MY HAIRSTYLIST, "I NEED SOME-THING *DIFFERENT*! I WANT *SHORT HAIR* LIKE MY BEST FRIEND MARJORIE!" AND THE NEXT MIN-UTE I HAD BEEN *BUTCHERED*! MY LIFE WAS IN A SHAMBLES...THROUGH THE TERRIBLE ACHE IN MY HEART, ONLY ONE THOUGHT CAME TO MY MIND, OVER AND OVER...

"I Hate My Hair!"

OH, MY GOD! I CAN'T *BELIEVE* THIS! I'LL HAVE TO GO INTO HIDING. I LOOK LIKE SINEAD O'CONNER.

MARJORIE HAD INVITED ME TO VISIT HER IN THE BIG CITY. I ARRIVED WEARING A NEW SUIT--COMPLETE WITH A MATCHING HAT TO COVER MY HORRIBLE HAIRDO...

I SHOULD TRY TO FIND ANOTHER SALON...

SUDDENLY, I HEARD A DEEP, WARM VOICE IN MY EAR...

EXCUSE ME, YOUNG MAN. YOU LOOK CONFUSED. CAN I HELP YOU FIND A TAXI?

WHAT? ARE YOU TALKING TO *ME?* CAN MY DAY GET ANY WORSE?

HE HAD MISTAKEN ME FOR A BOY! HADN'T HE NOTICED I WAS WEARING A SKIRT?...

THANKS. I THINK THE DRIVER CAN TAKE IT FROM HERE IF YOU WOULD GET YOUR HAND OFF THE WINDOW.

OKAY, SONNY, I GUESS YOU'RE ON YOUR OWN. GOOD LUCK!

MY HAT CAMOUFLAGE HAD CERTAINLY *FAILED!* I WAS SO UPSET BY THE ENCOUNTER WITH THE HANDSOME STRANGER I BARELY NOTICED THE SIGHTS OF THE CITY WHIZZING BY...

I SURE HOPE MARJORIE CAN DO SOMETHING WITH MY HAIR OR I'LL HAVE TO STAY INSIDE.

WHEN I GOT TO MARJORIE'S APARTMENT, SHE IMMEDIATELY TRIED TO MAKE ME FEEL BETTER...

OH, COME ON. IT'S NOT THAT BAD! YOU LOOK CUTE. IT GIVES YOU A KIND OF MILITARY MARY MARTIN LOOK.

I JUST WANTED TO LOOK MORE LIKE *YOU.* BUT THEY EVEN GOT THE *COLOR* WRONG!

HMMM. WE'LL HAVE TO DO SOMETHING ABOUT THAT *GARGANTUAN* BOW OF YOURS. IT MAKES YOUR HEAD LOOK *TINY.*

WHAT--SO NOW YOU'RE TELLING ME MY HEAD LOOKS LIKE A *TANGERINE*?

POOR DEAR--YOU *OBVIOUSLY* NEED A *DRINK.* WHICH IS FINE, BECAUSE I'M THROWING A *GREAT BIG* COCKTAIL PARTY TONIGHT! GO TRY TO *FLUFF* IT UP A BIT OR SOMETHING, WHY DON'T YOU?

THAT NIGHT I COULDN'T HELP FEELING A BIT SELF-CONSCIOUS, BUT MARJORIE WAS GOOD ABOUT INTRODUCING ME TO HER GUESTS...

AND HERE IS MY ALWAYS VERY *INTERESTING* AND *ORIGINAL* FRIEND FROM BACK HOME. GAIL, MEET MY NEW MAN, CLIFF ROBERTS.

WOW! THE BACK IS *SO ODD.*

OH, NO... IT'S *YOU!*

AND *YOU?*-- IN A *DRESS*?

2

EVERYONE AROUND STARTED LAUGHING. I TRIED TO LAUGH WITH THEM...

WHY, *CLIFF*, WHAT A BIZARRE THING TO SAY. WHAT DID YOU *EXPECT* HER TO WEAR? A *BIKINI*?

ACTUALLY, I THINK WHAT HE *EXPECTED* WAS A *COAT AND TIE.*

AFTER CLIFF TOLD THE STORY OF OUR CHANCE MEETING THAT AFTERNOON, MARJORIE REGALED THEM WITH DETAILS ABOUT MY HAIR SALON DISASTER. I BEGAN TO FEEL RESENTFUL...

SHE'S MAKING ME SOUND LIKE A COMPLETE IDIOT...AND SHE SURE HAS *CLIFF* ENTERTAINED!

THE NEXT FEW DAYS WERE AWFUL. I FELT I WOULD BE ALONE FOREVER. THE CITY WAS FULL OF LOVERS, LOVERS WITH *NORMAL* HAIR. WHAT IF MINE NEVER GREW BACK?

AT NIGHT I WATCHED CLIFF KISS MARJORIE...

...UNTIL I FELT I WOULD GO INSANE...

THIS IS A NIGHTMARE! I MAY AS WELL TEACH GYM!

AFTER FALLING ASLEEP I DREAMED THAT *I* WAS THE ONE IN CLIFF'S ARMS...THAT *I* WAS THE ONE HE WAS KISSING!...

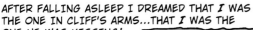

...AND WITH EVERY KISS, MY HAIR GREW AN INCH...

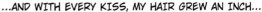

③

I HAD TO FACE THE FACT I HAD A SERIOUS CRUSH ON CLIFF. IT DIDN'T HELP THAT HE WAS UNDER FOOT ALL THE TIME, OFTEN STARING AT ME...

SWEETIE, I THINK IT'S TIME YOU CONSIDERED A **WIG** OF SOME SORT.

DON'T BE **SILLY.** I THINK IT'S QUITE **STRIKING.**

THE BACK IS SO VERY **BOYISH.**

THAT'S **ENOUGH!**

WHY DOES HE SOUND SO FASCINATED?

AFTER CLIFF'S COMMENT, I DECIDED TO SPEND THE DAY WITH MY BACK TO A TREE...BUT STILL HE SEEMED TO TAKE PERVERSE PLEASURE IN TEASING ME...

DOES SHE LOOK MORE LIKE MICHAEL J. FOX OR DOOGIE HOWSER?

WHY DON'T YOU GO DISCUSS IT SOMEWHERE ELSE AND JUST LEAVE ME **ALONE?**

WHEN THEY WERE GONE, I LET LOOSE ALL MY FRUSTRATION AND UNHAPPINESS...

I GOT SO DEPRESSED I TOOK TO MY BED. I ONLY SAW MARJORIE WHEN SHE CAME IN LATE FROM A DATE WITH CLIFF...

CLIFF WAS ASKING ABOUT YOU. "WHERE'S MY LITTLE ORANGE-HEADED TOMBOY?" HE KEEPS SAYING. I'M GETTING RATHER SICK OF IT.

YOU'RE SICK OF IT!!

SUDDENLY I FELT DESPERATE...

I'VE **GOT** TO TRY SOME NEW PRODUCTS--SOME COLORED MOUSSE OR SOMETHING...MAYBE EVEN **EXTENSIONS**...I'M GOING TO **SUE** THAT STYLIST...MY WHOLE LIFE IS **RUINED**...

THE NEXT MORNING, I WAS ABOUT TO TAKE A RAZOR TO MY SCALP WHEN THE DOORBELL RANG...

HOLD ON!

RING

④

I QUICKLY DONNED OLD SLACKS AND A T-SHIRT. MUCH TO MY DISMAY, IT WAS CLIFF AT THE DOOR...

PLEASE DON'T **LOOK** AT ME! I HAVEN'T SLEPT ALL NIGHT AND I'M DRESSED SCHLEPPY.

I **LIKE** THAT OUTFIT, GAIL. IT GOES WITH YOUR HAIR. YOU LOOK...WELL PUT-TOGETHER.

I DON'T KNOW IF HE WAS DRUNK OR WHAT, BUT HE FELL ASLEEP WHILE I WAS MAKING COFFEE...

I'M TEMPTED TO LOOSEN HIS CLOTHING.

AS I WATCHED CLIFF SLEEP, I THOUGHT ABOUT HOW I WOULD HAVE FLIRTED WITH HIM IF I STILL HAD MY HAIR, HOW I WOULD HAVE FLIPPED IT BACK A CERTAIN WAY WITH MY HANDS...

OH, MY SWEET **DARLING**, YOU'LL NEVER KNOW WHAT YOU'RE **MISSING**...

I WOULD HAVE TRAILED MY **LONG LOCKS** OVER YOUR CHEST, THOUGH SOME PEOPLE FIND THAT **ANNOYING**...

...AND YOU WOULD HAVE RUN YOUR **FINGERS** THROUGH IT, AND OKAY, MAYBE BY ACCIDENT YOU WOULD HAVE RIPPED SOME OUT, BUT IT WOULD HAVE BEEN **WORTH** IT...

...BECAUSE I LOVE YOU SO MUCH, AND NOW I'LL NEVER GET TO FEEL THAT BEAUTIFUL HAND OF YOURS ON MY HEAD...

I **SWEAR** I'M **SUING**!!

⑤

SUDDENLY I FELT THAT BEAUTIFUL HAND CLASPING MINE...

DON'T YOU GET IT, GAIL? I LIKE YOU JUST THE WAY YOU ARE!

HUH? DO YOU NEED TO SOBER UP, OR SOMETHING?

I'LL SOBER *YOU* UP, YOU LITTLE *MINX!* I'VE WANTED TO DO THIS EVER SINCE I SAW THAT CRAZY *CREW CUT* OF YOURS!

YOU REMIND ME OF THIS GUY I KNEW...

I WAS SO HAPPY--AND YET SO CONFUSED...

JOE WAS AN ARMY BUDDY— MY *BEST FRIEND.*

I'M NOT SURE I UNDERSTAND WHAT YOU ARE SAYING...

WHAT I'M *SAYING* IS THAT I HAVE BEEN LOOKING FOR A GIRL LIKE YOU FOR A LONG TIME...YOU'RE JUST MY *TYPE.* I DON'T LIKE LONG HAIR. I'D LIKE YOU EVEN BETTER IF YOU WOULD CUT YOUR *NAILS,* TOO.

WHATEVER. I JUST LOVE FEELING YOUR HAND ON MY HEAD.

6

WE WERE SO ENGROSSED IN EACH OTHER WE NEVER HEARD MARJORIE ENTER THE ROOM....

WELL, WELL. AT LAST, YOU HAVE FOUND A GIRLFRIEND WITH SHORTER HAIR THAN *YOU*! MAYBE YOU CAN GET "2 FOR 1" AT THE *BARBERSHOP*.

NEVER MIND, GAIL. I KNEW I WAS IN TROUBLE AS SOON AS I SAW THAT HAIRCUT OF YOURS.

CLIFF WAS THE ONE WHO MADE ME CUT *MY* HAIR. I WENT AS SHORT AS I DARED, BUT I COULD NEVER GIVE HIM THE *"BOY NEXT DOOR"* LOOK HE WANTED.

BUT LISTEN TO ME, GAIL. YOU'D BETTER THINK ABOUT IT *SERIOUSLY* BEFORE YOU COMMIT TO A WHOLE LIFE OF LOOKING LIKE *SANDY DUNCAN*.

I GAZED INTO CLIFF'S SEARCHING EYES. MY HEART ACHED FOR HIM BUT WAS I WILLING TO KEEP MY HAIR EXACTLY AS IT WAS NOW?...

THE ANSWER WAS *YES*!...

AS HE TOOK ME IN HIS ARMS, I KNEW I'D BE READY FOR A TRIM *SOON!*

⑦

From *Falling in Love* #9 (December 1956–January 1957). Illustrated by Tony Abruzzo and Bernard Sachs.

Original plot: As soon as she lays eyes on the dreamy substitute teacher at her secretarial school, Nan is smitten to the point of speechlessness. Nan is convinced the teacher is more interested in a fellow classmate until a car accident (brake failure) brings Nan and her teacher together in the end.

I HAD HEARD WAYNE ALLEN WAS BRILLIANT. WHEN I ENROLLED IN HIS FICTION WRITING WORKSHOP, I HOPED HE WOULD BECOME MY MENTOR...BUT ALL TOO SOON I LEARNED THAT HE HAD A PENCHANT FOR DUMB BLONDES AND NO USE AT ALL FOR...

My Heart of Darkness!

WAYNE'S SCHOOL
OF WRITING
FEMALE STUDENTS
HALF-PRICE

JESUS! HE CAN'T ACTUAL-LY *LIKE* THAT BIMBO!

AFTER TWO WEEKS OF CLASS I STILL DIDN'T FEEL READY TO SHARE MY WRITING, EVEN THOUGH MY FELLOW STUDENTS ENCOURAGED ME...

HEY!! YOU! *LOSER!* FRAIDY CAT!! HEY!! *FRAIDY CAT!!*

OH, NAN'S A *SERIOUS* WRITER! DON'T EVEN *TRY* TO TALK TO *HER!*

THEIR WORDS FELL AROUND ME LIKE DISTANT ACID RAIN. I WAS SO ENGROSSED IN MY WORK I DIDN'T NOTICE THE TEACHER, WAYNE, APPROACHING...

I WONDER IF THE CLASS WILL BE ABLE TO RELATE TO A WAR STORY.

SUDDENLY WAYNE WAS AT MY SIDE. HE URGED ME TO READ MY STORY, FINISHED OR NOT. THERE WAS SOMETHING ABOUT HIM THAT MADE ME WANT TO TRUST HIM...

OH, COME ON, HOW *SUCKY* CAN IT BE?

BUT I FELT MY CONFIDENCE FADE WHEN I HEARD THAT INSIPID, IRRITATING GIRL, MARSHA, BURST INTO HYSTERICAL LAUGHTER. SHE WAS ALWAYS LAUGHING AT EVERYTHING...

DOESN'T SHE REALIZE WE'RE ALL GOING TO *DIE?*

SUDDENLY WAYNE MADE A GRAB FOR MY NOTEBOOK. WE FOUGHT FOR IT, OUR FACES ONLY INCHES APART.... I THOUGHT I GLIMPSED DESPAIR IN HIS EYES, A *BLACK EMPTINESS* THAT MADE MY HEART LEAP...

STILL I REFUSED TO LET GO...

OKAY, UNTIL NAN IS READY, MARSHA CAN REREAD HER CHERRY FARM STORY. I COULD ALMOST TASTE THOSE PIES LAST TIME!

I CAN MAKE *REAL* PIES TOO!

②

THAT DID IT. I JUST COULDN'T STAND TO HEAR MAR- SHA'S SAPPY STORY AGAIN. SO I VOLUNTEERED TO READ MY WORK IN PROGRESS...

THE WORKING TITLE WAS "NUCLEAR MELTDOWN: THE END OF THE WORLD AND EVERYONE IN IT." AFTER ONLY A FEW PAGES, WAYNE INTERRUPTED ME...

WHAT **ARE** YOU? A DIS- GRUNTLED **POSTAL** WORKER!?

THERE WAS NERVOUS LAUGHTER FROM THE CLASS. I WAS STUNNED. HERE I HAD OFFERED ONE OF MY BEST EFFORTS EVER, AND WAYNE DIDN'T SEEM TO GET IT...

SO CAN I READ **MINE** NOW?

ABSOLUTELY! IT WILL HELP US ALL RECOVER FROM NAN'S **RANTING!**

AFTER CLASS ENDED I FELT SO HUMILIATED THAT I COULDN'T MOVE. I THOUGHT WAYNE WAS SUPPOSED TO BE A **REAL** WRITER. HOW COULD THIS BE HAPPENING? MARSHA, AS USUAL, HAD LINGERED BEHIND TO TALK PUBLISHING STRATEGY WITH HIM...

GOSH...DO YOU REALLY THINK READER'S DIGEST WILL TAKE IT?

AND THEN THE CLASSROOM WAS EMPTY EXCEPT FOR ME AND WAYNE....

WELL, MISS GLOOMY?

OH, **NO**--NOW MY LEGS ARE ASLEEP! I FEEL LIKE A PARAPLEGIC!

GETTING UP WAS AGONY. AL- THOUGH THE NUMBNESS AND PAIN IN MY LIMBS WAS KIND OF INTERESTING...

LIKE A ZOMBIE, I STAGGERED TOWARD HIS DESK...

③

HE TOLD ME MY CHOICE OF SUBJECT MATTER WAS MISGUIDED. THAT I WOULD NEVER GET PUBLISHED. THAT HE WAS GOING TO WORK HARD TO CHANGE MY WRITING STYLE...

HIS CRITICISM DIDN'T SIT WITH ME TOO WELL...

I HATE HIM.....I'D LIKE TO KILL HIM....

SOME KIDS FROM CLASS WERE WAITING FOR ME ON MY WAY OUT...

SO TELL US, NAN. ARE YOU A LONER? OR AN ANARCHIST?

WERE YOU TEASED AS A CHILD?

GET THE HELL AWAY FROM ME, YOU AIRHEADS!

I SAW WAYNE OUT ON THE STREET....

HE LOOKS DIFFER-ENT....

WAYNE SEEMED ODDLY MELAN-CHOLY, AND I COULDN'T HELP FOLLOWING HIM...

OKAY, NOW I'M A STALKER AS WELL.

WHAT I SAW WHEN I ROUNDED THE CORNER NAUSEATED ME. THERE WAS WAYNE--HAVING A TETE-A-TETE WITH THAT LAMEBRAIN MARSHA...

THE HORROR... THE HORROR...

I HAD A SUDDEN SPLITTING HEADACHE, WHICH USUALLY MEANT THE ONSLAUGHT OF A SUICIDAL EPISODE...

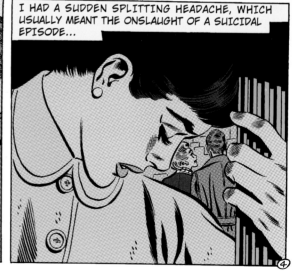

④

I WENT HOME AND SAT IN MY DARK BEDROOM. I GREW MORE AND MORE DEPRESSED...

WHY DO I HAVE THESE THOUGHTS? WHY CAN'T I WRITE STORIES ABOUT CHERRIES AND PASTRY LIKE MARSHA? MAYBE IT'S MY HAIR...THE COLOR OF BLOOD...I'VE GOT TO TRY TO CHANGE...

THE NEXT MORNING I SANG ONLY HAPPY SONGS...

...I'M AS CORNY AS KAN-SAS IN AUGUST...

...UNTIL I FELT LIKE A NEW WOMAN...

THAT *THREE-HOUR* SHOWER DID ME A WORLD OF GOOD. I HAVEN'T THOUGHT ABOUT DEATH *ONCE* SINCE BREAKFAST!

BUT AS SOON AS THE BELL FOR CLASS RANG AND I LOOKED INTO WAYNE'S EYES, I REALIZED NOTHING HAD CHANGED...

WELL HELLO THERE, LITTLE MISS END-OF-THE-WORLD!

RRRIINNGG!!

WAYNE WAS STILL GIVING ME A LOT OF GRIEF IN CLASS...

YOU'LL NEVER SELL ANY OF THAT SICK STUFF, YOU KNOW...

IT WAS GETTING HARDER AND HARDER NOT TO TAKE HIS CONSTANT HARANGUE PERSONALLY...

...NAN, JUST WHO DO YOU THINK YOU ARE--DOSTOYEVSKY?

HMMPH! WHO DOES HE THINK *HE* IS--ADOLF HITLER?

41

OUR ASSIGNMENT THAT DAY WAS TO WRITE A CHILDREN'S STORY. I FOCUSED EVERY FIBER OF MY CREATIVE SELF ON BEING UPBEAT...

OKAY. I CAN DO SWEET. I KNOW-- I'LL WRITE ABOUT MY PUPPY.

WAYNE WAS EAGER TO SEE WHAT I HAD WRITTEN...

NAN'S LATEST CREATION IS CALLED "THE STORY OF SNOWY THE SILLY SCHNAUZER." I HAVE TO ADMIT I'VE NEVER SEEN ANYTHING QUITE LIKE IT.

HIS EXPRESSION WAS HARD TO READ. HE HANDED MY STORY BACK TO ME...

I THINK THE CLASS WOULD ENJOY SEEING YOUR GREAT TRANSFORMATION. PLEASE READ THIS STORY ALOUD...

I READ THE WORDS I HAD WRITTEN WITHOUT THINKING, MY FACE FLUSHED, HOPING FOR THE APPROVAL OF MY TEACHER...

...LITTLE SNOWY WHIMPERED WHEN HIS MASTER DID NOT MOVE. BLOOD WAS OOZING FROM THE HEAD WOUND. THE LAST PERSON ON EARTH WAS DEAD AND--

WAYNE CUT ME OFF ANGRILY. IT WAS A FEW SECONDS BEFORE I REALIZED WHAT WAS HAPPENING, WHAT I HAD WRITTEN...

I'M SORRY, BUT YOU BELONG IN A DINGY CAFE IN PARIS, OR IN AN ASYLUM--NOT IN MY CLASS! THIS CLASS IS FOR PROFESSIONALS, PEOPLE WHO WANT A WRITING CAREER. FINISH THE WEEK--THEN YOU'RE *OUT!*

THE SHAME OF GETTING THROWN OUT OF WAYNE'S SCHOOL OF WRITING WAS SOMETHING I DIDN'T THINK I COULD SURVIVE...

I'LL NEVER WRITE AGAIN... I'LL CUT OFF BOTH MY HANDS...

6

LATER, WHEN I WAS WANDERING AROUND IN THE RAIN, I SAW WAYNE IN A LIP LOCK WITH MARSHA...

FIGURES.

I JUST COULDN'T BELIEVE I COULD BE SO WRONG ABOUT A GUY'S EYES...

HE SEEMED SO WONDERFULLY TORTURED WHEN I FIRST MET HIM!

SUDDENLY THE CLASS WAS PILING INTO MY CAR ALL AROUND ME...

DID YOU FORGET YOU OFFERED YOUR CAR FOR OUR CLASS TRIP TO THE BOOKSTORE?

OH, NO! I FORGOT ABOUT THE FUCKING FIELD TRIP!

THE OTHER STUDENTS STARTED GABBING ABOUT BEST-SELLERS. I HAD NEVER FELT SO LOW...AND THAT'S SAYING SOMETHING FOR ME...

OH MY GOD, I AM GOING TO THROW UP ON HER PAPAGALOS!

WITHOUT WARNING, WAYNE SLAMMED ON THE BRAKES...

EVERYBODY OUT! I CAN'T TAKE IT ANYMORE! I'M GOING TO *CRASH* THIS *BABY!*

COMPLAINING, THE OTHER STUDENTS CLIMBED OUT...

HE COULDN'T PICK A SUNNY DAY TO HAVE A NERVOUS BREAKDOWN?

⑦

BEFORE I COULD GET OUT, WAYNE TOOK OFF LIKE A ROCKET AND BEGAN TO DRIVE LIKE A MANIAC...

I FELL IN LOVE WITH YOUR BRILLIANCE THE VERY FIRST TIME YOU READ--YOU WRITE THE WAY *I* ALWAYS WANTED TO...

NOW YOU'RE MAKING ME BLUSH.

WE STARTED SKIDDING IN THE RAIN AND MUD. I'D NEVER FELT CLOSER TO ANOTHER HUMAN BEING...

A TRUCK CAME AT US AT HIGH SPEED. THIS WAS THE WAY I HAD ALWAYS PICTURED ROMANCE...

IT FEELS SO RIGHT TO RUN AMOK WITH YOU BE-SIDE ME...WHEEEEE!!

THE CAR TURNED OVER ONCE AND LANDED IN THE RIVER BESIDE THE ROAD. I FELT AS IF THIS WERE MY DESTINY, WHAT MY WHOLE LIFE HAD BEEN LEADING UP TO...

YOU'RE A GREAT WRIT-ER, BUT THE WORLD WOULD NEVER UNDERSTAND!

AS WE SLOWLY SANK, I FELT A HAPPINESS I HAD NEVER KNOWN...

I WAS SO JEALOUS OF YOUR TALENT. I *DESPISED* MARSHA AND THAT PIE STORY. I ONLY PRETENDED TO BE CHEERFUL-- BUT I ALWAYS LONGED TO DIE A TRAGIC DEATH IN THE RAIN!

OH WAYNE, I WAS RIGHT ABOUT YOU-- YOU'RE A KINDRED SPIRIT! YOU KNOW, I'VE WRITTEN ABOUT DROWNING BUT THIS IS BETTER--LIKE A DREAM COME TRUE...

AS THE RIVER ENGULFED US, OUR LIPS MET IN A LAST KISS. MY WORK WOULD DIE WITH ME, BUT AT LEAST IT HAD REACHED THE HEART OF THE MAN I LOVED!

The End

10 Ways to Get Over a Broken Heart

He's left you and your heart is broken! You feel as if you'll die of misery. Whatever you do, you can't stop thinking of him. You want the world to end right here and now!

But the world is *not* going to end and you are *not* going to die (well, you *might* die, but it will be of cancer or a car accident, or something like that). Remember that millions of girls have their hearts smashed to bits before they find their true love!

It isn't easy to forget about a boy you love who no longer loves you, but it *is* possible. Here are a few suggestions to help you get over your broken heart:

1. Have a good cry. This is the best thing to do right after it's ended. You'll feel much better afterward. Lock yourself in your room and rage at him out loud. Beat your fists on your dresser, rip out pieces of your hair, shatter expensive breakables. Fantasize about slitting your wrists, or taking a bunch of pills, or leaping off the Brooklyn Bridge. Wallow in self-pity until your friends begin to beg you to just go ahead and kill yourself already.

2. Start some new activity you never got around to before. Did you want to learn blues guitar? Now's the time to begin. Behind in your schoolwork? You can catch up! You're certainly not going out nights for a while. Are there dozens of books you've been meaning to read? Well, you've got the time for reading now, sister. You can become a real bookworm if you want. When you run out of novels, try reading the dictionary or the encyclopedia. It will give you a head start on conversation when you decide to start dating again.

3. Take up flirting. It will remind you that you are an attractive girl. Actually, having sex with a lot of other guys could be just the ticket to your feeling a *whole* lot better.

4. Don't be afraid to stay in some evenings. When you are used to going out every free night it can be hard to stay home at first. But if you don't let yourself worry about being a wallflower, you'll discover that relaxing by yourself can be very nice! Watching a lot of TV, for instance, can be quite soothing—especially when accompanied by eating large quantities of your favorite ice cream or cookies. After all, there's nobody looking, so you can pig out. You can also skip many annoying chores like cleaning the house, paying bills, and bathing. You may find a new kind of freedom!

5. Don't take revenge on other boys. Well, okay, maybe just a little. I mean, if you want to lead a couple of guys on, get them to fall in love with you, then drop them cold, who can blame you? Breaking another guy's heart isn't going to heal yours, but it might take some of the sting out of your wounded ego.

6. Spend more time with your girlfriends. Make a special effort to see the friends you neglected because you were too busy with *him*. Remember that friendship can—in a different way—be almost as satisfying as love. However, keep in mind that most of your girlfriends will be suspicious and resentful of your sudden interest in them when you haven't called them in months. You may have to pick up the check at dinner for a while (and be sure you order the sautéed crow).

7. Change your hairstyle or buy some new clothes. Doing something new with your appearance is a way of reminding yourself and others that a whole new life is beginning for you. You might want to start by having a ritual burning of everything you ever wore when you were with him. Then shave your head, get some new piercings and a tattoo that says "Love Survivor."

8. Do try to stay friends with him. A good way to do this is to hang around his house—say, across the street in a parked car with binoculars—and keep tabs on his every move. You can also call him a lot and hang up. Send him telegrams and anonymous letters—even dead animals if you like! Being friends with him will make you feel better about your breakup.

9. Look over the field carefully for new boys. Start by checking out all those guys you always thought looked interesting but never explored further because you had a boyfriend. Call them up and ask them for dates; tell them you have tickets for something and you were planning to take your boyfriend, but now you've broken up. If none of those boys will go out with you, ask a girlfriend to set you up on a blind date. Try the personal ads. Go to the grocery store and hang out in the cat food section. Train stations and bus stations are also good places to meet men. Get out there and mingle!

10. Don't let yourself think you'll never fall in love again. Don't let this experience cause you to lose hope about love. Don't start going to bars every night, drinking yourself under the table until the bartender has to pay someone to take you home. Don't become an obsessed career gal who delights in crushing male colleagues until their hair falls out. Don't move to a remote area and raise sheep. There are a lot of boys whose company you can enjoy and one day you'll meet one who will be right forever!

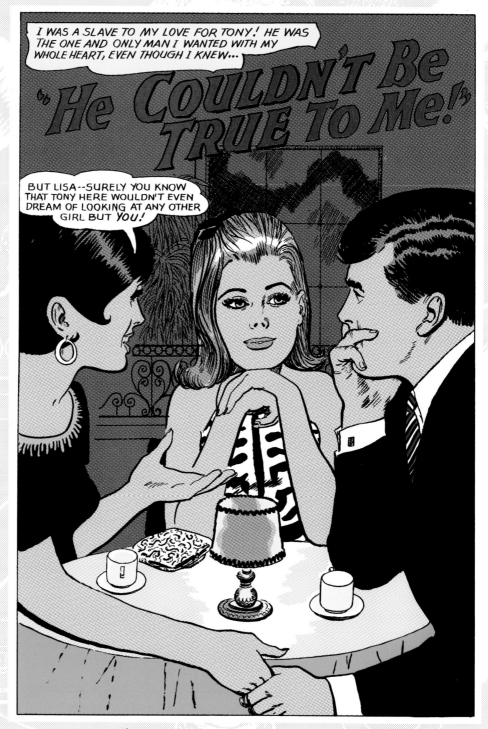

From *Girls Love Stories* #127 (May 1967). Written by Robert Kanigher and illustrated by Manny Stallman.

Original plot: When Lisa suspects her boyfriend, Tony, of having a roving eye, he manages to convince her it's just her paranoia. But when her cousin Irene comes for a visit, Lisa catches her secretly holding hands with Tony. Later that night, as the two girls are preparing for bed, Irene confesses she was faking the flirtation merely to prove once and for all to Lisa that Tony is a cad.

I HAD DATED TONS OF MEN--FROM SEXUALLY CONFUSED SINGLES TO MARRIED DON JUANS--WITHOUT MUCH LUCK...

THIS ONE IS SO LIGHT IN HIS LOAFERS!

HE'S NICE--FOR A CRACK-HEAD.

GOOD KISSER! TOO BAD HE'S MARRIED--

DAMN. A SCORPIO.

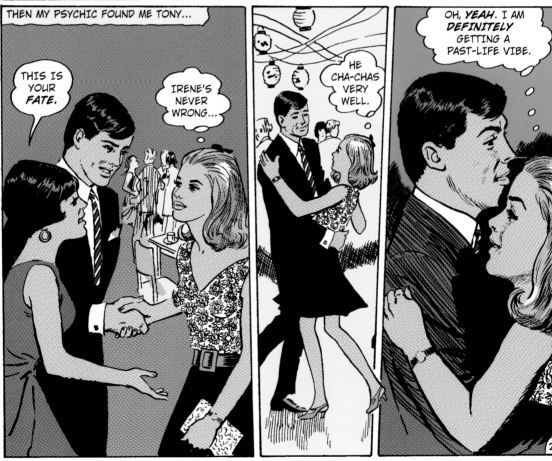

THEN MY PSYCHIC FOUND ME TONY...

THIS IS YOUR FATE.

IRENE'S NEVER WRONG...

HE CHA-CHAS VERY WELL.

OH, YEAH. I AM DEFINITELY GETTING A PAST-LIFE VIBE.

2

THE GOOD-NIGHT KISS PASSED THE TEST --IT WAS WALL STREET WITH A HINT OF TANTRIC YOGA...

FANCY TONGUE ACTION.

MY CHAKRAS WERE BUZZING...

YES!! NO MORE *MATCH.COM* FOR ME!

IT WASN'T UNTIL LATER THAT I REALIZED MY MISTAKE...

OH, MY *GOD*, I FORGOT TO TIP *IRENE*...

AND I DON'T HAVE HIS *NUMBER!*

NICE GOING, LISA! NO *WONDER* YOU'RE STILL SINGLE.

I DIDN'T GET MUCH SLEEP. PERHAPS THAT'S WHY I HAD SO MUCH TROUBLE DOING TELEPATHY THE NEXT DAY...

TONY...CALL *LISA...CALL LISA!*...

3

49

AT LAST HE CALLED--AFTER I PUT ON MY SIGNAL-BOOSTING CAP...

HI, TONY! I *KNEW* IT WOULD BE *YOU.*

THAT NIGHT WE WENT OUT ON OUR FIRST REAL DATE. IT WAS COSMIC...

I'VE HAD *EIGHT* YEARS OF COLLEGE, FOUR YEARS OF THERAPY AND *SIX* WEEKS OF YOGA.

I WAS SO GRATEFUL TO IRENE...

THANK *GODDESS!* MY SOUL MATE!

OF COURSE, TONY WAS NOT PERFECT, AS I BEGAN TO REALIZE AFTER DINNER...

TOUCH THAT PURSE AND I'LL CUT YOUR *DAMN HAND* OFF!

SORRY. BUT *I* PAY.

4

ACTUALLY, I HAD TO ADMIT WE DIDN'T SEE EYE TO EYE ON A LOT OF THINGS...

LOOK AT THAT HAPPY PAIR.

NICE-LOOKING LESBIANS!

THERE'S NO SUCH THING AS A *NICE-LOOKING* LESBIAN!

I WAS STUNNED...

THEY'RE RIGHT *BEHIND* US. HOPE THEY DIDN'T *HEAR* HIM.

SHE LOOKS OKAY TO ME.

I WAS BEWILDERED. HOW COULD MY SOUL MATE BE A GAY BASHER?...

OH, MY *GOD.* JUST WHO *IS* THIS GUY I'M WITH? WHAT MESSAGE IS THE *UNIVERSE* SENDING ME?

I TRIED TO MEDITATE IN THE CAR ALL THE WAY OUT TO NEW JERSEY. HERE WAS ANOTHER SHOCK: TONY WANTED TO LOOK AT **HOUSES**...

HOLD ON--DO YOU MEAN TO TELL ME YOU'D GIVE UP YOUR **TRIBECA** APARTMENT AND MOVE OUT HERE TO THE **SUBURBS?**

I'M TRYING **REALLY** HARD TO STAY OPEN TO THIS...

BUT I CAN'T **DO IT!** I'D RATHER DIE **ALONE** IN **MANHATTAN!**

TONY SMILED INDULGENTLY...

HONEY BUN, I'M THE ONE IRENE IDENTIFIED AS BEING YOUR **PARTNER** FOR THIS LIFETIME. SHE TOLD ME THERE'D BE DAYS LIKE THIS. RELATIONSHIPS TAKE **WORK.**

DON'T WORRY, MUNCHKIN. YOU'LL FEEL A LOT BETTER ONCE WE'RE MARRIED.

MARRIED? CAN'T WE JUST ...LIVE TO- GETHER? WAIT A MINUTE--

THE NEXT DAY, AT THE SKATING RINK...

TONY--WHY ARE YOU STARING AT THAT **GIRL**?

WHAT TONY SAID NEXT FLOORED ME...

IT'S JUST THAT I LIKE A WOMAN WITH BIG BREASTS. WOULD YOU EVER CONSIDER GETTING YOURS DONE?

YOU'RE KIDDING, RIGHT? **PLEASE** TELL ME YOU'RE KIDDING.

GEEZ. LITTLE MISS **NATURAL**! HAVEN'T YOU EVER HEARD OF A MAKE-OVER? LIGHTEN UP WHY **DON'TCHA**!

THAT'S IT! I AM **OUTTA** HERE!

HEY! LISTEN UP! OUR LOVE WAS MEANT TO BE! SO JUST **SHUT UP** AND **KISS ME**.

YOU TWO HUNGRY FOR SOME **FOOD**?

I CAN TELL YOU **EXACTLY** WHAT **THIS** LITTLE LADY WANTS.

7

I COULD NOT FIGURE OUT WHAT THE SPIRITS WERE TRYING TO TELL ME BY SENDING ME A MATE WHO WAS SO DISGUSTING. ONE DAY...

TONY'S TRYING TO PICK UP THAT GIRL!

THE SIGHT OF TONY'S PHILANDERING MADE ME FEEL SICK. I TURNED AND RAN...

I MUST FIND A LADIES ROOM!

BUT TONY CAUGHT UP WITH ME....

THE THING IS, I DON'T LIKE YOU.

I DON'T REALLY LIKE YOU ALL THAT MUCH EITHER--

BUT YOU THINK IT'S AN ACCIDENT WE BOTH LEFT THE HOUSE TODAY IN HATS?

DARLING, WE WERE DESTINED FOR EACH OTHER. IT'S WRITTEN IN THE STARS.

I DO LIKE THAT HAT.

⑧

BUT STILL I WAS HAUNTED BY DOUBT...

I JUST *CANNOT* IMAGINE EVER GIVING THAT MAN A *KEY*.

FINALLY I CALLED IRENE. I NEEDED HER INPUT...

CIAO. WHAT'S HAPPENING? YOUR AURA'S ALL WEIRD. YOU KNOW I'LL HAVE TO CHARGE YOU FOR THIS HOUSE CALL.

TO TELL THE TRUTH I *AM* CONFUSED--

ARE YOU SURE THIS TONY IS MY *SOUL MATE?* COULD YOU HAVE YOUR PSYCHIC WIRES *CROSSED* OR SOMETHING?

I'LL HANG FOR A WHILE.

AND SHE DID. THAT NIGHT...

DON'T KISS ME. COLD SORE, RIGHT HERE.

OKEY-DOKEY. WE'LL WAIT FOR THAT *COLD* SORE TO GET *WARM.*

GROSS! HE'S EVEN COMING ON TO IRENE!

I HAD ASKED TONY OVER FOR DINNER, AND IRENE STAYED TO OBSERVE...

HMM. THEY SEEM PRETTY CHUMMY. IRENE'S NEVER BEEN THAT WAY WITH *ME!*

9

IRENE MOVED IN WITH ME, EVEN THOUGH I KNEW IT WOULD COST ME A FORTUNE. THE NEXT NIGHT...

HEY. LET'S THE THREE OF US DO THE TOWN. YOU CAN EVALUATE US WHILE WE *PARTY DOWN.*

AH! I *KNEW* YOU WERE GOING TO SAY THAT. I'VE ALREADY MADE RESERVATIONS.

AND SO DANCE THEY DID...

IF SHE WOULD ONLY TALK TO HIM LONG ENOUGH...

SHE MIGHT *UNDERSTAND* WHAT A *CREEP* HE IS!

WHEN THEY CAME BACK TO THE TABLE, I DECIDED I MUST GIVE VOICE TO MY FEARS...

...AND HE SMOKES, AND I *KNOW* YOU SAY HE'S MY *TRUE LOVE,* BUT I'M HAVING TROUBLE *ACCEPTING* THAT--

HE *DID* DANCE WELL...

DANCING WITH YOU IS *HEAVEN--*

YES, I *RULE!* BUT I THINK NOW I SHOULD DANCE WITH IRENE.

I STILL HAVE A STRONG SENSE ABOUT YOU KIDS. LET ME FEEL HIS *ENERGY!*

10

I SAID I HAD TO PEE, THEN WATCHED FROM THE KITCHEN...

COME ON, IRENE...

I FELT LIKE A PRISONER WHO HAD JUST RECEIVED A LIFE SENTENCE...

I NEED *AIR*. I HAVE TO GO. I'LL CALL A CAB--

THE NIGHTMARE GOT WORSE, AS I HEARD IRENE SAY...

OH NO, WE'LL TAKE YOU. I *AM* STAYING WITH YOU. WE CAN DO SOME WORK ON THAT STUBBORN *HEART CHAKRA* OF YOURS.

WHEN I RETURNED I COULDN'T BELIEVE IT! IRENE SEEMED ENTHRALLED...

IRENE SAYS YOU'RE A LUCKY GIRL, THE *ONLY* GIRL FOR ME!

IT WAS SO AWFUL. THEY WERE WINKING AND JOKING...

AM I GOING *CRAZY*?

I HAVE BEEN TRYING TO TEACH YOU A LESSON ABOUT FREE WILL. AS IN, WHY DON'T YOU GET *YOURSELF SOME*, FOR PETE'S SAKE? THAT'S RIGHT, I'VE KNOWN ALL ALONG TONY'S NOT FOR YOU. THAT CREEP IS ACTUALLY MY *BROTHER.* I *HIRED* HIM TO DATE YOU.

I'VE LISTENED TO YOU FOR YEARS, TELLING ME ABOUT ALL YOUR MEN. BUT WHO WAS IT WHO ALWAYS DECIDED WHETHER HE WAS RIGHT FOR YOU? ME, THAT'S WHO!

SO WAIT...SO NOW I'M SUPPOSED TO TAKE YOUR ADVICE ABOUT *NOT* TAKING YOUR ADVICE?

I'M TRYING TO GET YOU TO TAKE YOUR *OWN* ADVICE, CHILD! I MEAN, WHY ARE YOU EVEN *WEARING* THAT SILLY ZEBRA DRESS? BECAUSE YOU ASKED *ME* WHAT YOU SHOULD WEAR!

B--BUT YOU'RE A *PSYCHIC!* IT'S NATURAL FOR ME TO BELIEVE WHAT YOU SAY. YOU CAN SEE THE *FUTURE!* SO OBVIOUSLY YOU'RE SMARTER.

WAIT, LET ME FEEL...

I THINK THERE *IS* A WAY, IF YOU WANT TO TRY IT, TO TRANSFER SOME OF MY PSYCHIC SMARTNESS TO YOU. WILL YOU TRUST ME ONE MORE TIME?

UM, OKAY.

SHE PLACED OUR CHESTS TOGETHER...

SO WHAT SHOULD I *DO*? ARE YOU *ALIGNING* OUR HEART ENERGIES? IS MY *HAIR* IN THE WAY?

JUST *RELAX.* EMPTY YOUR MIND.

IS IT WORKING?

IT'S STARTING TO. I CAN FEEL YOUR ENERGY SHIFTING A LITTLE. YOU'LL HAVE TO *REMOVE* THAT *DRESS.*

MY *DRESS*?

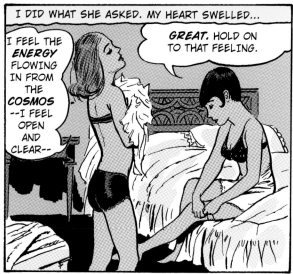

I DID WHAT SHE ASKED. MY HEART SWELLED...

GREAT. HOLD ON TO THAT FEELING.

I FEEL THE *ENERGY* FLOWING IN FROM THE *COSMOS* --I FEEL OPEN AND CLEAR--

TO BE TRULY *PSYCHIC*, YOU HAVE TO LET GO OF ALL YOUR PRECONCEPTIONS --OKAY?

WOW. IF THIS IS HOW IT FEELS TO BE PSYCHIC, *I LOVE IT!*

The End

14

THE MALE POINT-OF-VIEW

Dear Hank,

I met David on a blind date—the only one that ever worked out for me. I've dated him a few times and I'm really beginning to like him. How should I act? Should I tell him how I feel?

Timid Tammy

Dear Tammy,

Listen to me, kiddo. Never tell a man how you feel—ever. First of all they won't understand a word you are saying and secondly they couldn't care less. Wait, I take that back—if you tell them you feel sex-crazed, or hot to trot, or filled with insatiable desire, now that might hold their interest. And while we're at it, let me give you a tip, straight from the top-secret files of Hank "the Hunk" Hanson: Dress like you love them; but act like you hate them. Nice girls don't finish last, they are finished before they begin. So show your cleavage and your claws, kitten. I promise you'll be Prom Queen in no time.

Hank

♥   ♥   ♥

Dear Hank,

I'm a young woman of twenty with deep feelings for a young man of twenty-two. His feelings are not as intimate as mine so he tells me to slow down where my emotions are concerned. Can you really turn your feelings off? He wants me to know other people before I make up my mind as far as he's concerned. He wants me not only to do things

with *him*, but also a large part of it by myself. He feels this is an important part of growing up. He wants to do the same thing, to be sure of how he feels. However, I, as a woman, do not want to do this.

I feel that if he wants to do things with other women and see me, and just see me when he wants, I don't want any part of it. I can't have any part in a one-sided affair. I don't think he understands my feelings—he is just interested in having a "ball," while I, sure of my feelings, have to wait until he has had his share of women and fun.

Right or Wrong

Dear R or W:

Wake up and smell the prophylactics, baby. You, "as a woman," don't seem to know squat. Do you want him to draw you a diagram? The guy wants to play the field—hell, he is playing the field—and there you are still trying to throw a rope around him. And of course, like most females, you think having a serious discussion is the answer.

How dim-witted can you be? When a man starts talking about what is or isn't an important part of growing up, it can only mean one thing—you are history, darlin'. Yesterday's news. Off the table. Deleted off his hard drive. I swear, what do they teach you girls, anyway? How do you all ever hold down a job?

Sounds to me like you were easy pickin's, and now he's looking for a place to throw away the pit. If I've said it once, I've said it a thousand times: Feelings, schmeelings.

Hank

From *Falling in Love #1* (August–September 1955). Illustrated by Irv Novick.

Original plot: A woman on her way to rejoin her boyfriend gets stood up at the airport. The pilot of the plane she was just on pursues her and wins her love.

I KNEW THERE WAS GOING TO BE TROUBLE WHEN THE STEWARDESS BROUGHT THE PILOT BACK....

SHE HAD REPORTED ME FOR EXCESS CARRY-ONS. THE PILOT POLITELY INFORMED ME I'D HAVE TO CHECK SOMETHING NEXT TIME....

BUT THE STEWARDESS INSISTED I WAS OVER THE LIMIT AND HAD TO GET OFF THE PLANE...

I COULDN'T BELIEVE IT WHEN HE GAVE IN. I GOT A DEFINITE DOMINATRIX VIBE FROM THE STEWARDESS...

CAPTAIN

I COULD FEEL THE OTHER PASSENGERS' HOSTILE STARES BORING A HOLE IN THE BACK OF MY HEAD AS WE TAXIED BACK TO THE GATE....

I DON'T CARE WHAT THEY DO TO ME. I *REFUSE* TO CHECK ANYTHING!

THE PILOT AND THE STEWARDESS PERSONALLY ESCORTED ME OFF THE PLANE. HE TRIED TO MAKE ME FEEL BETTER....

YOU ARE REAL PRETTY. YOU HAVE A REAL NICE CHIN. CALL ME?

I'VE SEEN BETTER CHINS.

I FELT DAZED....AIRLINES HAD COMPLAINED ABOUT MY BAGS BEFORE BUT I HAD NEVER BEEN ACTUALLY THROWN OFF A PLANE.... I WASN'T SURE WHAT TO DO....

I HOPE THERE'S A BAR.

②

AFTER TWO MARTINIS THINGS LOOKED BETTER...

I THINK THAT PLANE IS SMILING AT ME.

UNTIL I HAD A REALLY TERRIBLE THOUGHT...

WHAT IF I END UP ACTUALLY HAVING TO CHECK A BAG?

I HAD NEVER FELT SO LOST AND SCARED...

CAN'T PEOPLE SEE THESE ARE FANCY SUITCASES? I JUST *KNOW* IF I CHECK THEM THEY'LL END UP IN THE TRUNK OF SOME AIRLINE WORKER'S DIRTY MUSTANG. OR IN SIBERIA, OR IOWA OR SOMEPLACE. THIS IS, LIKE, *SO* NOT FAIR!

THIS CAN'T BE HAPPENING. MAYBE IF I CLOSE MY EYES AND WISH REALLY HARD, I WILL STILL BE ON THE PLANE.....OKAY...THEY'RE PASSING OUT THOSE CRUMMY PRETZELS NOW...THE WOMAN BESIDE ME IS TELLING ME ABOUT HER HUSBAND'S ADDICTION TO SALTY FOODS...

SUDDENLY I SENSED SOMEONE BESIDE ME IT WAS THE PILOT! FOR ONE GLORIOUS, CRAZY MOMENT I THOUGHT HE HAD COME TO PUT ME BACK ON THE PLANE..

HERE YOU ARE, BAGS AND ALL! I FOUND MYSELF A SUB TO FLY THAT PLANE. I WANTED TO GET TO KNOW THE WORLD'S MOST *PIGHEADED* PASSENGER....WHAT HAVE YOU *GOT* IN THERE ANYWAY --GOLD DOUBLOONS?

I HATE IT WHEN MEN DON'T TAKE ME SERIOUSLY. I ALSO HATE IT WHEN THEY CALL ME "PIGHEADED." IN FACT, I PRETTY MUCH HATE MEN, PERIOD. I LASHED OUT AT HIM...

LISTEN, FLY BOY! IT SO HAPPENS THERE'S A *VERSACE DRESS* IN THIS SUITCASE...AND *EXCUSE* ME IF I DON'T PARTICULARLY WANT THE IDIOTS YOU CALL BAG HANDLERS PAWING THROUGH MY *UNDERWEAR!*

I HAD SAID "UNDERWEAR" OUT LOUD! I FLED...

SOMEBODY KILL ME!

I TRIED TO CALL MY LAWYER ON THIS WEIRD PHONE I FOUND INSIDE THE TERMINAL....

WHAT IS THIS? I CAN'T FIGURE OUT HOW TO WORK THIS STUPID THING. WHERE ARE THE BUTTONS?

FINALLY I GAVE UP AND WENT TO GET A CUP OF COFFEE TO SOBER UP A LITTLE....

GREAT. NOW I HAVE A DAYTIME HANGOVER.

THE LOUD CLANGING OF SOMETHING DROPPING ON THE TABLE STARTLED ME...

OKAY, LISTEN. I SWIPED THIS KEY TO YOUR SUITCASE AND HAD A LOOK-SEE. I HAVE TO ADMIT YOUR STUFF IS PRETTY DARN SPECTACULAR. I WAS PARTICULARLY IMPRESSED BY THE NUMBER OF CONDOMS YOU CARRY WITH YOU.

HE HAD UNCOVERED MY SECRET LOVE/HATE MAN THING...

SOMETIMES GIRLS HAVE NEEDS TOO. I LIKE TO BE PREPARED.

WELL, I KNOW IT'S NONE OF MY BUSINESS, BUT THE *GENTLEMAN* SHOULD TAKE CARE OF THESE THINGS. A PRETTY LITTLE GAL LIKE YOU SHOULDN'T HAVE TO BUY HER OWN.

I REALIZED THIS LIFT-OFF LOTHARIO COULD BE MY ALLY. SOMEONE WHO WOULD CUT THROUGH THE RED TAPE. SO I LET HIM HOLD MY HANDS...

...AND TURNED UP THE CHARM...

YOU KNOW, YOU HAVE VERY RONALD REAGAN-Y HAIR.

PEOPLE ALWAYS TELL ME THAT. BUT I LOVE HEARING IT.

④

I HAD TO TURN AWAY...

OH BROTHER! WHAT AN EGO. I CAN'T DO THIS.

JUST THEN I FELT A WET TONGUE PLUNGE INTO MY EAR...

THAT WAS JUST A FREE SAMPLE FROM MY SPECIAL STORE OF *SUPER JET-STREAM* LOVIN'. THERE'S MORE WHERE THAT CAME FROM, BABY. IF YOU PLAY YOUR CARDS RIGHT, I MAY HAVE ROOM IN MY *COCKPIT* FOR THOSE BAGS OF YOURS.

HIS OFFER WAS TEMPTING. BUT HE WAS SO *YUCKY.* I GRABBED THE KEY TO MY SUITCASE AND RAN...

I LOCATED A NORMAL PHONE AND TRIED TO CALL MY LAWYER AGAIN. BUT THE LINE WAS BUSY...

BUZZ! BUZZ!

I WAS FURIOUS. I'M AFRAID I TOOK IT OUT ON THE PHONE...

SLAM!

I WENT BACK OUTSIDE TO WHERE I THOUGHT I HAD LEFT MY BAGS. THEY WEREN'T THERE! HOW COULD I HAVE LEFT THEM UNATTENDED?...

WAIT...LET ME THINK....I WAS SITTING ON THEM, AFTER I HAD THE MARTINIS, THEN MR. JET STREAM CAME ALONG AND I TOOK OFF....HE MUST HAVE STASHED THEM SOMEWHERE!

5

SUDDENLY BEHIND ME I HEARD A FAMILIAR VOICE, FULL OF FURY. IT WAS THAT MEAN STEWARDESS...

LIKE TO KNOW WHERE YOUR PRECIOUS BAGS ARE, **SWEETIE**? I RISKED MY JOB TO STAY BEHIND AND **CHECK THEM** ONTO DIFFERENT FLIGHTS--EVEN THAT SILLY UMBRELLA! AND I THINK YOU KNOW WHAT CHANCE THAT HAS OF SURVIVING THE CARGO HOLD!

MY WORST NIGHTMARE HAD COME TRUE. SHE HAD CHECKED THEM-- THAT WAS BAD ENOUGH--BUT TO WHAT DESTINATIONS? FOR A FEW MINUTES I STOOD WHERE I WAS, UNABLE TO MOVE...

I FOUND MY WAY BACK TO THE PHONE. FOR SOME REASON IT WAS OUT OF ORDER. AND OF COURSE, THERE WAS THE PILOT, DOGGING ME LIKE THE RED BARON. I CLOSED MY EYES TO MAKE HIM GO AWAY. SOMETIMES THAT WORKS...

WHERE'D YOU GO, SUGAR? I WAS JUST GETTING WARMED UP. HEY! BETTER WATCH WHERE YOU'RE GOING!

PHONE BOOTHS

OKAY, SO THE CLOSED EYES DIDN'T WORK THIS TIME. I HAD TO OPEN THEM AND YELL...

LET ME TELL YOU SOMETHING, **MR. JOYSTICK**. THAT CRAZY STEWARDESS CHECKED MY BAGS! DO YOU UNDERSTAND ME? AND BY THE WAY, YOUR HAIR IS NOT ALL THAT RONALD REAGAN-Y. IF YOU WANT TO KNOW THE TRUTH IT'S MORE **GOMER PYLE-ISH**!

THE PAINED LOOK ON HIS FACE MADE ME WONDER IF I HAD GONE TOO FAR ABOUT THE HAIR...

I CLOSED MY EYES AGAIN AND STARTED RUNNING, NOT CARING WHERE...

⑥

I ENDED UP CRASHING INTO A METAL FENCE OUT ON THE TARMAC...

OWWW...MY HEAD!...I'M SO DIZZY ...I HEAR A HORRIBLE ROARING IN MY EARS....

A LUMP BEGAN TO FORM ON MY FOREHEAD...

WHAT AM I DOING? I'M ONLY RUNNING FROM THE TRUTH. PLUS I AM GETTING PRETTY BANGED UP IN THE PROCESS.

MY BAGS WERE GONE, MY PRETTY, PRETTY BAGS...

I FELT SOMEONE HOLDING ME CLOSE, CRUSHING MY THROBBING HEAD RIGHT INTO A WING-SHAPED PIN. STILL I REFUSED TO OPEN MY EYES...THIS HAD TO BE A DREAM...I WOULD WAKE UP SOON...

WEAKLY, I TRIED TO PUSH MYSELF AWAY FROM HIM, AWAY FROM THE IDEA THAT MY SUITCASES WERE REALLY GONE--ALONG WITH ALL MY MAKEUP. I FELT SOMETHING DIE INSIDE...

HE HELD ME TIGHTLY AS A STRANGE FEELING OF RELIEF CAME OVER ME...

DON'T YOU SEE? CHECKING *FREES* YOU.... YOU CAN RUN, CLOSE YOUR EYES, GET DRUNK...WITHOUT HAVING TO WORRY ABOUT WATCHING YOUR BAGS!

SUDDENLY I WAS SOARING UP, AS IF I WERE A PLANE, AN EXHILARATING AND UNFAMILIAR RUSH OF FREEDOM ENGULFING ME...

⑦

HE GRABBED ME VERY ROUGHLY. BUT I LIKED IT...

THAT'S IT, DARLING. DON'T THINK ABOUT YOUR BAGS. IF THEY ARRIVE THE SAME PLACE AS YOU, GREAT. IF NOT, DEAL WITH IT. PROMISE ME YOU'LL CHECK *ALL* YOUR LUGGAGE FROM NOW ON...

MAYBE I CAN KISS YOU INTO CHECKING...

I LET HIM KISS ME...ALL MY RESISTANCE WAS GONE...

JUST THEN I NOTICED A GROUP OF LAUGHING PEOPLE BOARDING A PLANE, COMPLETELY WITHOUT CARRY-ONS! AT ONCE I WAS FILLED WITH DOUBT...

BUT HOW *CAN* THEY?

THE PILOT COULD SEE I WAS WAVERING...

I SAW THAT. STOP IT.

I KNEW IT WASN'T GOING TO BE EASY TO SAY GOOD-BYE TO MY LIFE AS A CARRY-ON GIRL. BUT I WAS WILLING TO TRY...

WITH YOUR HELP, I'LL MAKE IT.

I WAS READY FOR MY NEW LIFE OF CHECKING MY BAGS. AND THIS TIME WHEN I FELT THE PILOT'S TONGUE IN MY EAR I DIDN'T GET GROSSED OUT.

THE END

A TEST OF TRUE LOVE

Will you know it when you meet your true love? He may set your heart a-thumpin' but how do you decide if he's really _the_ one? Take this quick True-False quiz to help you tell if it's _truly_ true romance!

1. You fell in love with him the second you saw him.

    ❏ T   ❏ F

(Answer: **True**. All true love happens at the first meeting. Love at first sight is the _forever_ kind of love!)

2. Some of his hair is blue.

    ❏ T   ❏ F

(Answer: **True**. If he has dark hair, and he probably does if he is your true love, you will notice a distinctive, royal blue sheen on parts of his head.)

3. When you kiss him, the skies open up, releasing a torrential downpour of blinding rain, which will affect neither your hair or clothing nor his.

    ❏ T   ❏ F

(Answer: **False**. This happens frequently, but not always. Sometimes when you kiss him there are just cartoon hearts floating around, or lots and lots of gulls. On the other hand, sometimes when you are merely thinking of him, it will start to pour. But there is a definite correlation between true love and rain.)

4. You have many things in common; you hold similar political beliefs and life values.

    ❏ T   ❏ F

(Answer: **False**. Are you kidding? The only topics you ever discuss are your romantic feelings, your exes, and maybe his job.)

5. When you leave your tiny boring Midwestern town to move to the city and start a new life as a famous singer, model or photographer, he shows up to convince you to move back home and become a homemaker.

    ❏ T   ❏ F

(Answer: **True**. He knows that a woman is only happy when she is the moon to his sun.)

6. When you cry over him, your tears always fall from your eyes as perfect beaker-shaped globules, which rest lightly on your cheek, never ruining your makeup and never turning your eyes red.

    ❏ T   ❏ F

(Answer: **False**. Often a kind of miniature waterfall tear will pour out over your bottom lid, and then stay suspended there for a really long time. However, it _is_ true that your makeup will never run, ever.)

7. You see birds everywhere—seagulls, crows, robins, swans—in the sky, on the windowsill, flying around your car, night and day.

    ❏ T   ❏ F

(Answer: **False**. This is not strictly true. While there will probably be birds around you, if yours is a case of true romance, you and your true love will never even notice them. Even when a huge blue jay is perched outside your office window or flocks of terns are swarming over your head.)

8. When you are lying in your bed tossing and turning and thinking of _him,_ a disembodiment of his head will often appear and sail around over your bed.

    ❏ T   ❏ F

(Answer: **True**. This allows you to talk to your true love when he is not really there. It also allows him to see you in your jammies.)

9. You never run out of interesting things to say to each other.

    ❏ T   ❏ F

(Answer: **False**. That is, you have no way of knowing, as you have few long conversations. On dates you either go to drive-ins or loud discotheques, or spend the evening kissing beside a tree.)

10. Whenever you are outside together at night, your entire bodies—including your clothing—turn a pale blue color.

    ❏ T   ❏ F

(Answer: **True**. Isn't it lovely?)

If you got eight or more of the answers right, give him a close-up kiss and live happily ever after! He's your _truly_ true love!

From *Young Love* #85 (March–April 1971). Written by Jack Oleck and illustrated by Art Saaf.

Original plot: Convinced that she has fallen out of love with the dull, hardworking Steve, Sue steps out with exciting party guy Lou. Unfortunately, at the mere mention of marriage, Lou splits. Sue is overjoyed when dull, hardworking Steve comes back to her.

LOOK, *SUSAN*, WE JUST WENT OUT TO A FABULOUS RESTAURANT. WE SAW A GREAT PLAY. DON'T TELL ME YOU ARE GOING TO RUIN OUR EVENING *AGAIN* WITH YOUR *WORK PROBLEMS*?

YOU DON'T UNDERSTAND HOW *AWFUL* IT IS. IT'S LIKE THE *NAZIS*!

IT'S NOT JUST THE *TYPEWRITERS*. IT'S THE *NEW RULES*. WE HAVE TO SHOW A PICTURE I.D. TO GO TO THE *RESTROOM*!

AND THE *SHIT* WORK! THEY'VE TURNED ME INTO A STUPID ROBOT. MY BRAIN IS *GONE*.

FOR CHRIST'S SAKE, SUSAN! IF IT'S THAT BAD, THEN WHY DON'T YOU *QUIT* THE DAMN JOB? I AM *SO SICK* OF THIS WHINING.

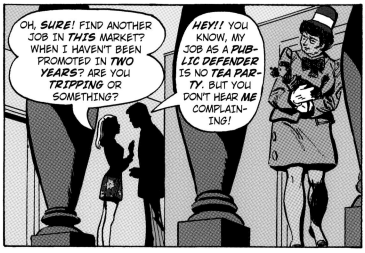

OH, *SURE*! FIND ANOTHER JOB IN *THIS* MARKET? WHEN I HAVEN'T BEEN PROMOTED IN *TWO YEARS*? ARE YOU *TRIPPING* OR SOMETHING?

HEY!! YOU KNOW, MY JOB AS A *PUBLIC DEFENDER* IS NO *TEA PARTY*. BUT YOU DON'T HEAR *ME* COMPLAINING!

POKE ME WITH A FORK. I'M *DONE* WITH THIS RELATIONSHIP!

2

AFTER STEVE LEFT I WENT TO A CLUB TO BLOW OFF STEAM. I DID SOME MAJOR DRINKING, DRUGGING AND DANCING...

AND I HOOKED UP WITH THIS WILD, TOTALLY COOL GUY NAMED LOU. I REALLY FELT I COULD LET MY HAIR DOWN WITH HIM...

OH, LOU, I FEEL SOOO *NICE*. ISN'T THIS *NICE*? YOU FEEL *NICE*. EVERYTHING'S *NICE*!

I KNOW HOW TO FEEL EVEN *NICER...*

MMM...IF YOU ONLY KNEW THE *ASSHOLE* I STARTED THIS NIGHT OUT WITH. I WAS TRYING TO TELL HIM ABOUT HOW MUCH MY *JOB* SUCKS, AND HOW I HATE MY *BOSS*--

SAY, WHAT?

NOTHING. JUST THAT I WORK AT THIS *VILE* PLACE AND I--YOU KNOW, NEED TO *VENT*.

WHOA! HOLD IT *RIGHT THERE*, ANGEL. DON'T EVEN *THINK* ABOUT TALKING ABOUT YOUR HARD DAY AT THE OF-FICE AROUND *ME!*

BUT, LISTEN--WE HAVE THESE *1970'S* TYPE-WRITERS THAT--

LOOK! I HAVE MY *OWN* STUPID ROTTEN JOB TO OBSESS ABOUT. I DON'T NEED TO HEAR ABOUT *YOUR* STUPID ROTTEN JOB.

NOW TELL ME WHERE YOU LIVE SO I CAN TAKE YOU HOME.

3

THAT NEXT DAY AT WORK MADE ALL OTHER DAYS LOOK LIKE HONEYMOONS IN BALI. I HAD LOST STEVE FOREVER, THE ANTIQUE RIBBON ON MY TYPEWRITER WAS BROKEN AND I HAD A VICIOUS HANGOVER. BUT SUDDENLY...

BAD DAY?

I LEAPT OUT OF MY CHAIR AND INTO STEVE'S WAITING ARMS. THE SUDDEN MOVE MADE ME WANT TO VOMIT, BUT I DIDN'T MIND...

STEVE!! I'LL NEVER COMPLAIN ABOUT MY JOB AGAIN. *I LOVE YOU!* I LOVE *OLD TYPE-WRITERS!* THEY --THEY MAKE A GREAT *SOUND!*

CHILL, DOLL. I GUESS YOUR *SUCKY JOB* IS A PART OF WHO YOU ARE. ANYWAY, I THINK I MAY BE ABLE TO *HELP!*

OH, STEVE! WHAT IS *THAT*? OH, MY GOD, YOU FOUND ME A *NEW* JOB, DIDN'T YOU!!

ARE YOU *CRAZY*? IN THIS *MARKET*? BESIDES, WHAT CAN YOU DO? YOUR COMPUTER SKILLS ARE TOTALLY *ATROPHIED*. YOUR SELF-ESTEEM IS *GONE*. BUT I HAVE SOMETHING THAT MIGHT HELP.

I STARED AT THE PAPER HE HELD OUT. AT FIRST I COULDN'T EVEN UNDERSTAND WHAT IT MEANT. ALL I KNEW WAS IT HAD MY NAME ON IT...

I FINALLY SAW THAT YOUR *INCESSANT BITCHING* WAS REALLY A CRY FOR HELP. SO I PULLED A FEW *STRINGS DOWNTOWN*. IT WASN'T EASY!

THEN HE BENT ME BACK OVER THE DESK, RIGHT THERE IN THE OFFICE...

THAT MAN OF MINE WAS ONE IN A TRILLION! IF I WANTED PROOF OF HIS LOVE I HAD IT NOW, IN BLACK AND WHITE!...

GRAND JURY SUMMONS: REPORT IMMEDIATELY FOR JURY DUTY TO...

End

DEE PRESSEN
Love Counselor

Dear Dee,

I've known Hal for a few years and I've been secretly in love with him all this time. He was going steady with another girl, though, and she jilted him about three months ago. After their breakup he started taking me out. He says he enjoys my company a lot, but yet he acts very moody when we are together. Although he denies that he is still in love with the other girl, I am pretty sure he hasn't forgotten her. He wants to continue going out with me but not on a steady basis.

I don't know what to do. Shall I keep seeing him on the chance that his feelings for me will change? I am twenty years old and I don't know if it is wise to get involved in a romance which may never lead to anything serious and will keep me from meeting other boys.

Insecure

Dear Insecure,

So. You like him but he likes someone else. You are confused and feeling unloved. Welcome to life on Planet Earth.

Of course Hal is moody. Like everyone else he is desperately searching for something he will never find. And don't worry too much about being twenty. Whatever your unhealthy predilections and patterns are with the opposite sex, believe me they are not going to change much. Get used to it. In fact it will only get harder, as you go through life falling in love over and over again and having your heart broken so much you feel like a piece of glued-together secondhand crockery. True love is a myth they teach little girls and boys in Disney movies. The truth is, we are born alone, and we die alone; life is hard, and then you die.

My advice to you is to go ahead and keep seeing this boy. Eventually he will dump you, and then you will have to go meet some other boys. But for the time being, at least this Hal is a warm body. It's not like Mr.

Right is waiting out there, so why not date Mr. Right Now?

Dee

♥   ♥   ♥

Dear Dee,

I am an average girl of fifteen who likes to go out with fellows. I am on the heavy side and am quite self-conscious about it. I mean I'm a wallflower at parties. I never dance with any of the boys. I try so hard to go on a diet but I don't succeed.

I wouldn't care that much if I wasn't invited to parties, but I am. I also have gatherings in my house very often. My friends have all the fun while I sit in the kitchen. I make up excuses to them that I can't dance because I don't want them to know I am self-conscious. (I really can't dance with boys very well.) When my girlfriends come to my house we usually play records and dance. I am not ashamed to dance with them; in fact, they say I dance pretty well. Please try to help me. I'm very downhearted about everything....I am 5'3" and weigh 145 pounds.

Unhappy

Dear Unhappy,

You seem like a very astute girl—obviously very perceptive and more mature than the rest of your friends. Eating too much is a very practical way to handle the harsh realities of life and is certainly better than suicide. What your fat is doing is protecting you from getting close enough to a boy so that he can break your heart. Good for you! Your survival instincts will serve you well throughout your life. Keep it up.

Dee

From *Heart Throbs* #60 (June–July 1958). Illustrated by Seymour Barry and Bill Draut.

Original plot: In this odd Swan Lake/Cinderella tale, the insecure Lora falls in love with her brother's friend Alex, while believing Alex could only love her more sophisticated older sister. The heroine gets the guy when she finally gives up trying to act like the sister and decides to be herself—a sweet girl who happens to love talking to a swan.

MY TOTAL LACK OF A LOVE LIFE HAD BEEN REALLY DEPRESSING ME. IT DIDN'T HELP WHEN MY HOUSEMATE BILL BROUGHT HIS NEW BOYFRIEND OUT IN THE GARDEN TO MEET ME...

THIS IS THE GUY I TOLD YOU ABOUT!

BEFORE I KNEW WHAT I WAS DOING, I WAS SHAKING THE HAND OF THE MOST GORGEOUS HUNK I HAD EVER LAID EYES ON...

HELLO. I'M ALEX. AND YOUR NAME IS...?

MY *NAME*?...MY NAME. UM--OH. IT'S--LORA.

IT WAS MORTIFYING! I WAS SO INTENSELY ATTRACTED TO THE MAN THAT I COULDN'T MOVE OR SPEAK...

OH, YOU'VE *GOT* TO BE KIDDING. MY GOD, THIS ONE *CAN'T* BE GAY!

MY FACE MUST HAVE GIVEN ME AWAY, FOR SOON I NOTICED A TEASING, KNOWING LOOK IN BILL'S EYES...

DARLING! YOU OKAY? NEED TO *COOL OFF* INSIDE?

I FELT LIKE SUCH AN IDIOT. WHAT WAS WRONG WITH ME...?

WHY IS EVERY MAN I MEET PLAYING FOR THE *OTHER TEAM*? I'VE GOT TO GET *OUT* OF THIS LO-CAL DECAF CAPPUCCINO TOWN!

I WATCHED BILL AND ALEX AS THEY WALKED BACK TO THE HOUSE. THEY BOTH HAD SUCH NICE BODIES. IT JUST WASN'T FAIR...!

BILL FINDS TRUE LOVE ONCE A WEEK. AND *ME*? LEFT OUT HERE TO PRUNE *ROSES*. WHAT IS WRONG WITH THE UNIVERSE? WHAT IS WRONG WITH *ME*?

2

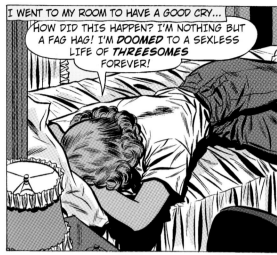

I WENT TO MY ROOM TO HAVE A GOOD CRY...

HOW DID THIS HAPPEN? I'M NOTHING BUT A FAG HAG! I'M *DOOMED* TO A SEXLESS LIFE OF *THREESOMES* FOREVER!

THEN A REALLY SCARY THING OCCURRED. I SAW ALEX'S HEAD...

IT WENT UP AND FLOATED NEAR THE CEILING. IT WAS LOOKING DOWN AT ME AS IF IT WERE GOING TO START TALKING.

I MUST HAVE SCREAMED BECAUSE BILL CAME TO SEE WHAT THE MATTER WAS...

WHAT IS GOING *ON*, GIRLFRIEND? DO *NOT* TELL ME YOU'RE HAVING ONE OF YOUR LITTLE *EPISODES*. I NEED YOU TO BE RELATIVELY SANE. I'M GOING OUT OF TOWN AND I WAS HOPING YOU'D KEEP ALEX COMPANY.

THIS SEEMED A BAD IDEA, CONSIDERING THE FLOATING HEAD...

OH, COME ON, ROOMIE. BE AN ANGEL! HE THINKS YOU'RE *FABULOUS*! AND I'D LIKE YOU TWO TO GET TO *KNOW* EACH OTHER.

RELUCTANTLY, I AGREED. THOUGH MY HEART TOLD ME IT WAS A MISTAKE...

LOOK. HE'S GREAT COMPANY. AND I DON'T WANT SOME OTHER MAN POACHING ON MY LAND WHILE I'M GONE.

SURE, BILL. I'LL DO IT.

AFTER HE LEFT, I GAVE MYSELF A PEP TALK IN THE MIRROR...

GET A *GRIP!* YOU CAN *DO* THIS!....UH-OH. WHY CAN'T I SEE MY LIPS MOVING?

③

I DECIDED TO MAKE THE BEST OF THINGS. AFTER ALL, WHAT WAS SO BAD ABOUT BEING SQUIRED AROUND BY A HANDSOME MAN...?

IT WON'T HURT TO TRY TO LOOK MY BEST. I MEAN, YOU NEVER **KNOW** WHAT CAN **HAPPEN** WITH THE RIGHT **OUTFIT**...

I PUT ON A REAL GLAM SUIT, WITH MY VINTAGE GLOVES AND A KILLER HAT I HAD BEEN SAVING FOR A SPECIAL OCCASION..

I AM SO PRETTY! WHAT MAN COULD RESIST THESE BUTTONS!

I MADE QUITE AN ENTRANCE COMING DOWN THE STAIR-CASE. I FELT MY FASHION EFFORTS WERE APPRECIATED...

HEY, WOW! IT'S TIPPI HEDREN!

IT'S **WORKING**! ALEX THINKS I'M GOOD-LOOKING! MAYBE HE'S JUST NEVER MET THE **RIGHT GIRL** BEFORE.

WE TOOK BILL TO THE STATION AND THEN WENT TO EXPLORE THE CITY. IT FELT SO RIGHT SITTING BESIDE ALEX IN THE CAR--AND YET, SO WRONG.

I'M SITTING TOO CLOSE. HE KNOWS I LIKE HIM. HE FEELS MY HAND ON HIS KNEE.

IT WAS AT THE BOTANICAL GARDENS I STARTED TO FEEL REALLY EMBARRASSED..

HE KNOWS I'M AFTER HIM. HE'S **LAUGHING** AT ME!

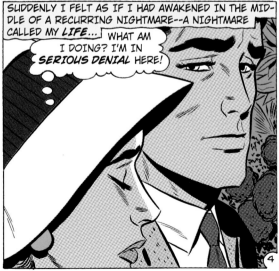

SUDDENLY I FELT AS IF I HAD AWAKENED IN THE MID-DLE OF A RECURRING NIGHTMARE--A NIGHTMARE CALLED MY **LIFE**...

WHAT AM I DOING? I'M IN **SERIOUS DENIAL** HERE!

4

NEXT WE WENT TO THE ZOO. MY SELF-ESTEEM WAS SO LOW BY THEN I STARTED OVERCOMPENSATING...

LOOK AT THAT MONKEY, ALEX. HE'S *STARING* AT ME! HE THINKS I'M *SEXY*, DON'T YOU THINK?

LATER, AT THE LAKE IN THE PARK...

...SO BILL AND I WANT TO BUY A *BEACH HOUSE*...

HELLO THERE, MR. SWAN! DO YOU THINK I AM *ATTRACTIVE*? I LIKE YOUR LONG NECK. COME OVER HERE AND GIVE ME A *LITTLE KISS*, MR. SWAN!

SUDDENLY I REALIZED WHAT I WAS DOING. I WAS FLIRTING WITH A SWAN! I TURNED MY HEAD AWAY IN SHAME BUT COULD FEEL ALEX'S LOOK OF PITY. HE COULD SEE ALL MY LONELINESS AND DESPAIR...

BECAUSE HE WAS SUCH A SWEET GUY, HE KISSED ME ON THE CHEEK. ACTUALLY I WOULD HAVE RATHER HE PUNCHED ME IN THE STOMACH...

THIS IS *TORTURE*. I MUST HAVE DONE SOMETHING *REALLY BAD* IN A PAST LIFE.

THAT NIGHT I HAD THIS VERY WILD SEX DREAM INVOLVING A BIG BLACK SWAN. ALEX WAS IN THE DREAM TOO, BUT IT WAS MOSTLY ABOUT THE SWAN...

5

AS IF THINGS WEREN'T BAD ENOUGH, ALEX DECIDED HE WANTED TO CHECK OUT THE LOCAL BEACH THE NEXT NIGHT. AND OF COURSE IT WAS A MOONLIT, ROMANTIC NIGHT...

OKAY, NOW THIS IS *HOSTILE*. WHAT CAN ALEX BE THINKING? IS HE *TRYING* TO DRIVE ME OVER THE EDGE?

WE WALKED ALONG THE SHORELINE, THE WATER LAPPING AT OUR FEET LIKE AN IRRITATING BEGGING DOG...

IF HE TELLS ME ONE MORE THING ABOUT HOW WONDERFUL *BILL* IS, I WILL PUSH HIM INTO THAT *BEACH GRASS* OVER THERE. I *SWEAR* I WILL.

WHEN I COULDN'T BEAR BEING NEXT TO HIM ANY LONGER, I WENT FOR A RUN--BY MYSELF...

ON THE WAY BACK IN THE CAR, I REALIZED WITH HORROR THAT I HAD COMPLETELY RUINED A $200 PAIR OF HEELS...

WE HAD ANOTHER HOUSEMATE, NITA, WHO WAS JUST BACK FROM EUROPE. SHE WAS SO MUCH MORE WELL ADJUSTED THAN I WAS...

ALEX! BILL SENT ME A POSTCARD ABOUT YOU. HOW NICE OF YOU TO *INDULGE* OUR LORA. SHE HASN'T GOTTEN OUT MUCH--NERVES, YOU KNOW.

NITA'S WORDS CUT ME TO THE QUICK. WITH HER WIT AND SUPERIOR ATTITUDE, SHE SWEPT ALEX AWAY FROM ME...

MY GOD, YOU MUST MISS *BILL* LIKE CRAZY. I KNOW HOW *NEW LOVERS* CAN BE. BEEN SEEING ANY OTHER MEN OR HAVE YOU BEEN A *GOOD BOY*?

THAT NIGHT NITA FOUND ME ONCE AGAIN SOBBING ON MY BED, RAILING AWAY AT GOD FOR MY DATELESSNESS...

OH, NITA, I JUST CAN'T STAND IT ANYMORE. IT'S ONE *GAY MAN* AFTER *ANOTHER.* I JUST DON'T WANT TO GO ON LIVING!

BUT NITA HAD LITTLE PATIENCE FOR MY SUFFERING...

WAKE UP AND SMELL THE COFFEE. WE'RE OVER THIRTY. OF *COURSE* THE SINGLE ONES ARE GAY. WHAD'YA WANT, A BLOODY MIRACLE?

I KNEW NITA WAS RIGHT. WHY COULDN'T I ACCEPT IT? I TOOK A PILL THAT NIGHT SO I COULD GET A GOOD NIGHT'S SLEEP BUT STILL I DREAMED ABOUT THAT SEDUCTIVE SWAN...

HEY, *BABY.* GET OVER HERE.

I CAN KISS LIKE A *HUMAN!*

IN THE MORNING I WAS STILL KIND OF IN A SWAN-INDUCED DAZE...

HELLO! EARTH TO LORA! LOOK, MY MUDDLED LITTLE SWEETIE-PIE, THERE'S A *DANCE* TONIGHT AT THE CLUB. YOU MIGHT AS WELL COME. ALEX INVITED US. HE'S A *GREAT* DANCER!

I KNEW WHAT NITA WAS SAYING WAS WISE. BUT SOMETHING IN ME REBELLED...

I DON'T WANT TO GO. I LOVE ALEX.

HONEY, YOU LOVE *ALL* BILL'S BOYFRIENDS. YOU WANT ANOTHER *BREAKDOWN?*

7

EVENTUALLY I DID DECIDE TO GO TO THE DANCE. BUT IT TOOK FOREVER TO PICK OUT WHAT TO WEAR...

FOR SOME STRANGE REASON I REALLY WISH I OWNED A *FEATHER BOA*...

AFTER MUCH SOUL-SEARCHING--AND EVEN MORE TRYING ON OF DRESSES--I MADE UP MY MIND NOT TO GIVE UP ON MY SEARCH FOR TRUE LOVE. MAYBE I COULD MEET SOMEONE NEW, SOMEONE WONDERFUL...

THERE'S ALWAYS MARRIED MEN...

BUT WHEN I ARRIVED I FOUND I WAS A LITTLE SHAKY IN THE CONFIDENCE DEPARTMENT. I THOUGHT I WOULD JUST FIX MY MAKEUP, WHEN SUDDENLY THERE WAS NITA...

WHO ARE YOU PRIMPING FOR, *SILLY?* DO YOU THINK THERE ARE *STRAIGHT GUYS* HERE?

THE PAIN OF REALITY WAS TOO GREAT. I TURNED AND RAN, WITHOUT THINKING WHERE I WAS GOING...

I AM NOT DOING THIS ANYMORE! THIS IS TOO *FRUSTRATING!*

MY FEET FOUND THEIR WAY TO THE LAKE. AND HE WAS WAITING FOR ME, AS HE HAD BEEN IN MY DREAMS...

HELLO, MR. SWAN! WILL YOU PLEASE HOLD ME IN YOUR ARMS...OR ER, WINGS?

8

AS HE PRESSED HIS BEAK TO MY LIPS, I KNEW THAT MY DREAMS OF LOVE HAD ALL COME TRUE. HE WAS EVEN STARTING TO LOOK A LITTLE LIKE ALEX TO ME...

YOU ARE THE MOST DESIRABLE WOMAN IN THE WORLD. I LOVE YOU WITH MY *WHOLE BEING.* I'M SO GLAD YOU CAME TO CLAIM MY SWAN'S HEART. THERE'S JUST ONE THING: I'M AFRAID OUR LOVE CAN *NEVER* BE *PHYSICALLY CONSUMMATED!*

WELL, THAT'S NOTHING NEW!

The End

Dear Dotty

Dear Dotty,

A girlfriend of mine gave my name to a fellow I never met who lives in another state, and he has been writing to me. He seems nice enough from his letters, and I enjoy reading them and writing back. But for a long time my mother objected to the correspondence. I told her there was nothing wrong with it and continued to write to and receive letters from this boy.

Then I stopped getting letters. Now I have found out that my mother has been ripping them up before I can even see them. What can I do about this?

Angry

Dear Angry,

I myself once got a letter from a boy I knew in high school. He was such a nice boy. He told me he had become a salesman in a hardware store. Or was it a national hardware store chain? I don't remember exactly, but I was so very glad to hear from him. My mother always liked him, and she always said to me that he would make a good husband. But I never got married. I was engaged once, to a nice man I met at a dinner party my friend, Sue, gave. I remember we had squab.

I like getting letters. Don't you? You should keep writing them, and just ignore the whole e-mail trend.

Dotty

♥ ♥ ♥

Dear Dotty,

For two years I went steady with a boy just a few months older than me. We didn't get along too well, so we broke up. Then we got back together again and now I know it was a big mistake. He has no respect for other people and he uses awful language. Although he is trying to get me back again, I am avoiding him.

My problem is that now I like a boy who is a year older than I am. He is everything a girl could want in her boyfriend. He shows respect for girls. He is polite and gentlemanly and is very neat about himself. I am crazy about him and I think he likes me, although we only see each other about every two weeks because we live in different towns. He is tall, fine, and terribly sweet.

My problem is this: should I allow myself to get really interested in him? I am afraid to get really involved for fear it will be another mistake. I am pretty sure it wouldn't be, but I want to avoid either of us from getting hurt. Should I stay away from him so that he will lose interest in me or should I take a chance?

"Daredevil"

Dear Daredevil,

"Taking a Chance on Love" is a wonderful song. I loved it when Ella Fitzgerald sang it. She had such a great voice, even when she was just doing Memorex commercials. It always shocked me to see her in those funny glasses, though. I think those glasses may have been a mistake. I wonder if she picked them out or her manager did.

You go out with as many boys as you want, dear, and have a good time. Get your young men to take you to some jazz concerts.

Dotty

From *Girls Love Stories* #133 (February 1968). Illustrated by Howard Purcell.

Original plot: Scarred by early heartbreak, Brenda has developed a bad habit of stringing two or more boyfriends along at once; that is, until the handsome Dr. Roger Wheeler comes along. Roger forces Brenda to confront her past, thereby curing her of her polygamous propensities and at the same time rendering her completely in love with him.

AS A GIRL I WAS CONFIDENT. AND IT WASN'T BECAUSE PEOPLE FLATTERED ME-- I *KNEW* I WAS SPECIAL...

YOU'VE GOT BETTER POSTURE THAN WE DO. YOUR HAIR HANGS WELL.

STOP IT, BETTY. YOU'LL GIVE BRENDA A SWELLED HEAD.

DON'T WORRY. I ALREADY *KNOW* I'M AWESOME.

I REMEMBER MY VERY FIRST DATE. IT WAS WITH THIS GUY NAMED BRIAN WHO WAS A FRIEND OF BETTY'S...

YOU TWO HAVE A LOT IN COMMON.

WOW.

WOW.

I FELT SO COMFORTABLE WITH HIM--I HAD NONE OF THE NERVOUSNESS A GIRL USUALLY FEELS ON HER FIRST DATE...

I COULD GO FOR YOU IN A BIG WAY, BRENDA.

WE MAKE A GOOD COUPLE.

...OR ON HER FIRST KISS...

I BET WE LOOK GREAT DOING THIS.

2

THAT NIGHT, AS I WAS POSING IN FRONT OF MY MIRROR...

HOW COULD HE *NOT* LOVE THIS *BOD*?

IT'S LIKE I'VE KNOWN HIM *FOR-EVER*!

THE NEXT DAY I WAS DO-ING MY SOCIAL SCIENCE HOMEWORK WHEN I CAME ACROSS A SECTION ON "NARCISSISM"...

HMM...THIS SOUNDS KIND OF FAMILIAR.

THAT'S WHEN THE REALIZATION HIT ME...

...*I WAS A NARCISSIST*!...

I LIKED *BRIAN* BECAUSE HE...LOOKED LIKE *ME*!...

I CAN'T SEE HIM AGAIN-- IT'S LIKE DATING *MYSELF*!

HE KNEW JUST HOW TO SWEET-TALK ME...

I KNOW I'M GORGEOUS, BUT STILL IT NEVER SEEMS *ENOUGH.*

I KNOW HOW YOU *FEEL,* BABE. I ALSO KNOW WHAT YOU *THINK.* I KNOW WHAT YOU HAD FOR *BREAKFAST...*

BEFORE I KNEW IT, I HAD AGREED TO GO OUT WITH HIM...

I WONDER IF I'M SLIPPING...I WONDER WHAT I'LL WEAR...

SOON I WAS IN LOVE...

--OH, BRENDAN, *I KNOW*...THE WAY OUR EYELASHES ARE SO DARK AND CURLY, AND THE WAY OUR EYEBROWS ARCH--

WHO WAS THAT ON THE PHONE? *PLEASE* TELL ME IT WAS YOUR SISTER.

IT...IT WAS BRENDAN. HE LOVES ME SO!

YOU TWO MAKE ME SICK!

6

HEY! WHAT ARE YOU DOING WITH MY DRESS?

TAKING IT! AND LEAVING.

IN FACT, I'M TAKING **ALL** YOUR CLOTHES. I DESERVE THEM JUST FOR HAVING TO **LISTEN** TO YOU!

YOU'RE SO **CONCEITED!**

I CAN'T HELP IT.

--AND NO **OUTFITS EITHER!**

THEN SHE WAS GONE...

DARN! NOW THERE'S NO ONE TO TRY ON MY OUTFITS IN FRONT OF!

⑦

AFTER BRANDY LEFT, I BECAME MORE OBSESSED...

HE LOVES ME...*I* LOVE ME... HE LOVES ME...*I* LOVE ME...

I STARTED LOOKING FOR BRENDAN EVERYWHERE...

I *KNOW* HE'S GOT TO GO IN THERE AT SOME POINT TODAY.

◀ MEN

EVENTUALLY I FOUND HIM...

DARLING, WANT TO READ ALOUD TOGETHER?

YES, PLEASE!

WE SOUND GREAT.

AT THE FOOTBALL GAME, WE WERE TOO BUSY TALKING TO EACH OTHER TO WATCH THE PLAYERS...

SO--I THOUGHT I'D TRY MOUSSING MY BANGS...

THAT REMINDS ME--THE PHOTO LAB SAID MY *SELF-PORTRAIT* IS DONE...

BRENDAN OPENED HIS HEART TO ME...

THE THING ABOUT **ME** IS, OKAY, YES, I DO EVERYTHING VERY WELL, AND PEOPLE **ADMIRE** ME AND ALL--

--BUT STILL I NEVER REALLY FEEL LOVED--I NEVER FEEL **CONNECTED**, YOU KNOW?

CAN I HAVE FRIES?

I KNOW **ONE** THING THAT MAKES ME FEEL LESS HOLLOW...

KISSING IN PUBLIC!

THE NEXT DAY I WAS HANGING OUT WITH BRITT, THE R.A. IN MY DORM...

DO YOU *EVER* LISTEN TO ME?

OH, BRITT! I LISTEN *FINE*. DIDN'T I HEAR YOU JUST NOW WHEN YOU TALKED ABOUT MY EATING SHELLFISH?

SHE ENCOURAGED PERSONAL GROWTH...

YOU SEE? THIS IS WHAT I MEAN. WHAT I WAS TALKING ABOUT WAS YOUR *BEING SELFISH.*

OH. I GUESS YOU HAVE A POINT. I'M *NOT* A GREAT LISTENER. IT'S FUNNY, BECAUSE I'M GREAT AT SO MANY OTHER THINGS...

BUT MOSTLY I WOULD STARE AT MY UPPER ARM AND DREAM OF MY BEAUTIFUL BRENDAN...

YOU KNOW, FREUD SAID THERE WAS NO CURE FOR NARCISSISM. THAT FREUD KNEW HIS STUFF.

I FELT SO *ALIVE* WHEN I WAS WITH BRENDAN...

BRENDAN AND I MIGHT HAVE GONE ON HAVING MEANINGLESS FUN TOGETHER FOREVER...IF IT WEREN'T FOR AN UNEXPECTED ACCIDENT...

I HAD GONE TO BUY SOME MORE OUTFITS TO REPLACE THE ONES BRANDY HAD TAKEN, WHEN SUDDENLY...

YOU IDIOT!

I'M NO IDIOT.

WHAT THE CLUMSY BUT HANDSOME STRANGER SAID NEXT SHOCKED ME...

I'M BRAD--A *NARCISSIST*, LIKE *YOU*. I'VE SEEN YOU AROUND TOWN, WITH THAT PRETTY BOY, BRENDAN.

WHY DON'T YOU COME TO A MEETING TONIGHT? IT'S IN THERE.

NARCISSISTS ANONYMOUS

YOU MEAN TALK ABOUT *MYSELF* IN FRONT OF *STRANGERS*?

11

NO, THAT'S THE TRICK. WE'RE SUPPOSED TO TALK ABOUT *OTHER* PEOPLE.

I MAY BE BUSY.

ALL DAY LONG I COULDN'T STOP THINKING ABOUT BRAD. THERE WAS SOMETHING ABOUT HIM...

HE TALKED CRAZY, BUT I *LOVED* HIS EYES...

BEEP! BEEP!

I STOPPED IN TO SEE BRITT...

SORRY...I KNOW YOU SAID NEVER TO COME IN WITHOUT KNOCKING, BUT I'VE HAD THE MOST EXTRAORDINARY DAY AND I *KNEW* YOU'D WANT TO HEAR ABOUT IT!

THAT EVENING, I SAW BRENDAN...

WE LOOK JUST LIKE THOSE MOVIE STARS!

SHE DIDN'T SEEM ALL THAT THRILLED TO SEE ME....

BRITT? NO, SHE'S BUSY RIGHT NOW.

UH...MY PHONE?

BUT THAT NIGHT, I DREAMED I WAS KISSING BRAD...

I LOVE YOU IN YELLOW.

I LOVE YOU IN RED.

I TRIED TO BE HAPPY WITH BRENDAN AND IGNORE THE LURE OF BRAD ...

I AM THE KING OF EARTH!

I'M THE QUEEN!

BUT THE NEXT DAY I WAS DRAWN BY SOME MYSTER-IOUS FORCE TO THE N.A. HEADQUARTERS. WHAT I DIDN'T KNOW WAS THAT *BRENDAN* HAD FOLLOWED ME!...

WELCOME TO *N.A.*, BRENDAN. YOUR GIRLFRIEND IS ALREADY HERE.

BRENDA! DON'T TELL ME YOU FELL FOR THIS *PSYCHOBABBLE?*

13

14

BRITT HEARD ME SOBBING IN MY ROOM AND CAME OVER TO SEE WHAT WAS GOING ON...

OH, BRITT! I'M SO **SICK** OF ME! I DON'T WANT TO SEE MY FACE ANYMORE. I THOUGHT BRAD WAS THE ANSWER, THAT THINGS WOULD BE **DIFFERENT**--

I **HATE** MY LIFE! I THINK I NEED TO BECOME A BUDDHIST OR SOMETHING...

WHEN ALL MY TEARS WERE SPENT, I LEFT THE DORM, NOT CARING WHERE I WAS GOING, EXCEPT THAT I FIGURED I WOULD TRY TO FIND A BUDDHIST COLONY...

BRENDA-**BABY!**

BEFORE I KNEW IT I WAS IN BRAD'S PERFECT ARMS...

YOUR FRIEND BRITT CALLED AND SAID YOU WERE **FREAKING**. BRENDA, YOU'RE TOO **HARD** ON YOURSELF. WE **ARE** NARCISSISTS. WE'LL **ALWAYS** WANT OTHERS TO BE OUR MIRRORS--

WE'RE **ALWAYS** GOING TO WANT TO BE SHOW-OFFS AND TO DAZZLE THE REST OF THE WORLD WITH OUR TALENT AND BEAUTY...

FORGET BUDDHISM! NOW, COME ON, BRITT'S WATCHING. LET'S MAKE THIS GOOD!

The End

15

From *Young Romance* #161 (August–September 1969). Illustrated by Jack Sparling and Vince Colletta.

Original plot: High school sweethearts Brian and Cheryl are separated when Brian gets drafted and sent to Vietnam, where he is shot in the face. Thinking Cheryl can now have nothing but pity for him, Brian tries to dump her via mail. She comes to see him in the hospital and convinces him that she will love him no matter what his disfigurement is after the plastic surgery.

THE NEXT DAY I WORE MY VERY BEST PLAID AND STRIPED COMBO FOR HIM. I EVEN BLEW OFF MY CLASSES TO SEARCH FOR HIM IN THE HALLS...

AT NIGHT I RACED THROUGH MY HOMEWORK SO I COULD PLAN MENUS FOR US. MY MOTHER HAD TAUGHT ME THAT GUYS MY AGE ONLY HAD ONE THING ON THEIR MINDS—FOOD...

WHERE ARE YOU, MY LOVE? I WANT TO START *COOKING* FOR YOU!

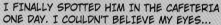

I FINALLY SPOTTED HIM IN THE CAFETERIA ONE DAY. I COULDN'T BELIEVE MY EYES...

WHAT IS HE DOING WITH *ANOTHER GIRL*?

I MADE A BEELINE FOR THEIR TABLE. I HAD BOUGHT A LUNCH I THOUGHT HE WOULD LIKE, JUST IN CASE...

WHO'S THE BABE WITH THE BOOBS?

HELLO! I BROUGHT YOU WHAT I HOPE ARE ALL YOUR *FAVORITES*...

I DIDN'T KNOW THERE WERE *WAITRESSES* HERE!

2

THAT WAITRESS COMMENT STUNG ME. BUT I DIDN'T GIVE UP. I TALKED OVER MY PROBLEM WITH MY BEST FRIEND, SUE, EVEN THOUGH SHE WAS A BIT OF A DOOM-AND-GLOOM GIRL...

HIS NAME IS **BRIAN**. HE ALWAYS PASSES BY HERE ON HIS WAY HOME FROM FOOTBALL PRACTICE. BUT **GIRLFRIEND**, HE'S KNOWN ALL OVER SCHOOL AS A **PLAYER**--A REAL HIT-AND-RUN ARTIST. YOU SURE YOU--?

LET'S **TACKLE** HIM!

GET THE HELL OUT OF MY WAY!

NO! YOU'RE COMING FOR A **SODA**.

HOW DOES BRIAN GET HIS HAIR LIKE THAT?

IT'S COMBED FORWARD.

MAYBE HE PUTS **MOUSSE** ON IT AND HANGS HIS HEAD OVER.

HOW DO YOU LIKE THIS GUY? ALL HE DOES IS LOVE 'EM AND LEAVE 'EM, AND **STILL** NO GIRL CAN RESIST. HEY **SUE**, HEY **CHERYL**: HOW ABOUT **LOOKING** AT ME WHEN I'M **TALKING**?

BUT BRIAN'S TEAMMATE DIDN'T EXIST FOR ME. I ONLY HAD EYES FOR BRIAN. I COULDN'T BELIEVE HOW **FINE** HE WAS. I JUST HAD TO MAKE HIM REALIZE I WAS HIS **DESTINY**...

I'LL BUY HIM ANOTHER SUNDAE.

LOOK AT THIS CHICK, DUDE! SHE'S SO FAR GONE OVER YOU SHE DOESN'T KNOW WHERE SHE **IS**!

WHEN I WENT HOME THAT AFTERNOON I WAS ON CLOUD NINE! HE HAD ASKED ME OUT! WELL, MAYBE NOT DIRECTLY, BUT HE HAD SAID HE OFTEN BIKED THROUGH MY NEIGHBORHOOD...

OKAY THEN! CATCH YOU LATER. GOTTA RUN...UM ...ER...**CHERRY**!

IT'S **CHERYL**!

3

THAT SATURDAY I FIXED THE MOST INCREDIBLE PIC-NIC YOU EVER SAW--EVERYTHING FROM MACADAMIA NUTS TO CHEESECAKE. THEN ALL I HAD TO DO WAS TO WAIT BY THE WINDOW FOR A FEW HOURS UNTIL BRIAN CAME BY...

I DIDN'T KNOW YOU LIVED HERE...

DON'T BE *SILLY!* I'M ALL READY!

IT WASN'T EASY CARRYING THE BULKY PICNIC BAS-KET ON MY HANDLEBARS. BUT I WANTED TO SHOW BRIAN WHAT A FUN DATE I WAS...

SO WHERE SHALL WE GO, *BRI?* I BET YOU HAVE SOME ROMANTIC SPOT ALL *SCOPED OUT.* WANNA RACE ME DOWN THIS HILL?

UH--I'LL GIVE YOU A HEAD START.

WOW! SPECTACULAR CRACK-UP!!...

CRASH!

IT'S OKAY. I SAVED MOST OF THE *FOOD.*

COOL! BECAUSE I MADE IT JUST FOR YOU...I GUESS YOU COULD SAY I FELL *HEAD OVER HEELS*--HEE-HEE...

SUDDENLY HE WAS STARING AT ME LIKE I WAS A BIG, JUICY STEAK. MY BUTT HURT FROM THE FALL AND I HAD A SPRAINED WRIST BUT I DIDN'T CARE...

I *AM* HUNGRY...

THEN HE KISSED ME! I KNEW OURS WAS A LOVE TO LAST FOREVER AND SO I LET MYSELF BE SWEPT AWAY, EVEN THOUGH WE WERE REALLY ONLY TEN MINUTES INTO OUR FIRST DATE...

H

LOST IN OUR PASSION, WE SORT OF FORGOT WE WERE IN A PUBLIC PLACE...

I THINK WE SHOCKED SOME OF THE SQUIRRELS...

...BUT I KNEW THAT THERE WAS NO SUCH THING AS GOING *TOO* FAR WHEN YOU ARE WITH THE MAN YOU ARE GOING TO *MARRY*...

AFTER THAT I NEVER MISSED A FOOTBALL PRACTICE OR A GAME. I TOOK GOOD CARE OF BRIAN'S EVERY NEED...

THANKS, *CHERRY.* THESE ARE GREAT. BUT NO MORE AFTER THIS. I'VE STILL GOT *HALF A GAME* TO PLAY.

THEY'RE *HOMEMADE.* I STUFFED THE *CASINGS* BY HAND.

I LOVED TO WATCH HIS EYEBROWS WHEN HE DRANK...

5

THEN, ONE EVENING...

BRIAN, WHAT'S THE *DEAL?* I CAN TELL SOMETHING IS WRONG. WE HAVEN'T BEEN TO *AL'S MOTEL* FOR LIKE, A WHOLE WEEK. ARE YOU MAD AT ME?

CHERRY, WE NEED TO TALK.

IT'S *CHERYL*, HONEY.

THIS HAS BECOME A REAL *BORE*.

WHAT?

THIS. US. YOU AND ME. FOR ONE THING YOU JUST DON'T SEEM TO *GET IT* THAT I PLAY THE *FIELD!* THIS IS JUST FOR *KICKS.* AND FOR ANOTHER THING, I AM GAINING SO MUCH DAMN *WEIGHT* FROM YOUR CONSTANT FORCE-FEEDING THAT SOON I WON'T EVEN BE *FIT* FOR BABE HUNTING!

OH, SWEETIE! I'VE READ ENOUGH ABOUT THE *MARS/VENUS* THING TO KNOW NOT TO TAKE YOU LITERALLY. OUR LOVE IS SO BIG I KNOW IT CAN BE SCARY. BUT I'M NOT FRIGHTENED. I'LL *NEVER* LEAVE YOU, DON'T WORRY.

I MUST SAY I WAS SURPRISED WHEN BRIAN SUDDENLY ANNOUNCED HE HAD ENLISTED IN THE MARINES. BUT IT WAS A GOOD TEST FOR OUR LOVE. I WAS SURE THE SEPARATION WOULD MAKE OUR BOND STRONGER. BRIAN HID HIS PAIN WELL WHEN I KISSED HIM GOOD-BYE...

I'LL BE HERE, WAITING.

BRIAN SENT ME A VERY SERIOUS LETTER FROM OVERSEAS. BUT I KNEW MY DARLING WAS JUST TRYING TO PROTECT ME...

"PLEASE DON'T TAKE THIS TOO HARD, CHERRY, BUT WE ARE NOW *OFFICIALLY BROKEN* UP. IT WAS FUN BUT IT'S DONE, OKAY? DON'T SEND ME ANY MORE FOOD! MOVE ON, KIDDO. *I* HAVE."

6

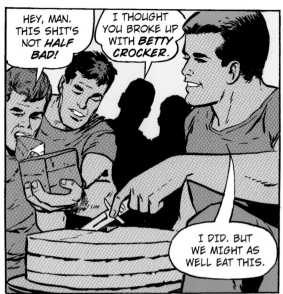

ABOUT A WEEK LATER, I RECEIVED AN ANSWER...

HE'S IN A BASE HOSPITAL IN FRANCE. THERE'S SOMETHING HERE ABOUT AN "ALCOHOL-RELATED" MISHAP." ...HE WAS SHOT BY A FELLOW GI! ALCOHOL? THE POOR DARLING MUST HAVE REALLY MISSED ME!

DOES IT SAY THAT ANYWHERE? HELLO? EARTH TO CHERYL! DIDN'T YOU GET A "DEAR JANE" LETTER TWO MONTHS AGO?

YOU DON'T UNDERSTAND OUR SPECIAL BOND. BRIAN MAY SAY HE DOESN'T LOVE ME, BUT I KNOW WHAT HE REALLY MEANS IS THAT HE LOVES ME DEEPLY. LIKE WHEN HE SAYS HE DOESN'T WANT SECONDS.

I BAKED A FEW GOODIES AND FLEW OVERSEAS TO SEE HIM...

BRIAN! I'M HERE, MY LOVE!

NMMMPH! NMMPH, MMPH MMPH, NMMPH, NMMPH...MMPH MMPH MMPH MMPH! RUMMPH, RMMPHS! RMMPHS!

MMPH! NA-NMMPH, MMPH MMPH, NMMPH, NMMPH ...MMPH MMPH MMPH MMPH! HRUMMPH, RMMPHS!

TAKE IT EASY, I KNOW WHAT YOU ARE TRYING TO SAY. YOU THINK BECAUSE YOUR FACE HAS BEEN RUINED, THAT WILL CHANGE MY LOVE FOR YOU!

LISTEN TO ME, SWEETHEART. I'VE GOT A HOUSE PICKED OUT FOR US. IT HAS A GREAT KITCHEN. WE'RE GOING HOME AND GETTING MARRIED JUST AS SOON AS WE CAN!

I DON'T THINK THAT'S SUCH A GOOD PLAN, LADY. THERE'S SOMEONE HERE TO SEE YOU. FOLLOW ME, AND BRING THAT MUMMY WITH YOU.

CHERYL, THIS IS JOE AND HIS SISTER, MARY. JOE WAS THE GI WHO ACCIDENTALLY SHOT BRIAN'S FACE OFF. SOME SORT OF RUM CAKE THING. I BELIEVE THEY HAVE SOMETHING TO TELL YOU.

CHERYL? I THOUGHT IT WAS CHERRY. OH WELL. LOOK! YOU AND BRIAN ARE HISTORY. HE'S TOLD YOU, I'M TELLING YOU--AND NOW MY SISTER MARY CAN TELL YOU. SHE AND BRIAN ARE ENGAGED. AND SHE CAN'T COOK AT ALL, THANK GOD!

I TOLD YOU THAT GIRL SCARES ME, JOE! LET GO!

OKAY, SO A GIRL CAN BE WRONG ABOUT TRUE LOVE SOMETIMES! BUT IT WAS ALL FOR THE BEST, BECAUSE ON MY WAY OUT OF THE HOSPITAL I MET MY SOUL MATE...!

OH, TOM, I'M SO GLAD I FOUND YOU AT LAST! OURS IS AN ETERNAL LOVE! DINNER?

THE END